Discover Birds

Written and Illustrated by Ian Wallace

Photographs by Philip Sayer

Foreword by Sir Peter Scott

Whizzard Press/André Deutsch

Published by Whizzard Press
in association with André Deutsch Ltd., 1979
105 Great Russell Street, London WC1

ISBN 0 233 97100 9

Printed in England by W. S. Cowell Limited
Filmset by Oliver Burridge & Company Limited
Colour separation by Printing House Reproductions Limited

Contents

Foreword by Sir Peter Scott

In 1952 Ian Wallace's father arranged a supply of small trout for our fish-eating ducks at Slimbridge. Taking up my invitation to see our waterfowl collection and the first of that winter's wild geese, the Wallace family arrived on a fine October morning. Like many of his generation, the son's enthusiasm for every bird that moved was so consuming that within minutes a tantalising warbler had Ian Wallace as lost in our decoy wood as any duck. In the last twenty-seven years, Ian has watched birds from the Pacific Coast of Canada to deepest Baluchistan, and has become an amateur field ornithologist of international standing. Though most of his time is given to the fishing industry, Ian has somehow found enough to spare for writing on many bird subjects from identification to population dynamics. His contributions to the journal *British Birds* have been particularly appreciated and his initials DIMW have become well known under beautifully accurate and evocative vignettes and plates. Above all, Ian has coupled with his lasting sense of wonder at birds an ability to communicate it to others.

I welcome *Discover Birds* as one of the few recently published books which captures the spirit of bird watching. The photographs by Philip Sayer skilfully conjure up the great bird places and their inhabitants. He should have good reason to be pleased with his first essay in natural history photography, which is liberally complemented by line drawings and coloured plates by Ian himself, derived from hundreds of field sketches.

Bird-watching is happily a growing pastime for thousands of people, and this is a book to trigger off a flying start and lasting enthusiasm. Ian has written it as a passport to the world of birds and I can confirm that it will take you into it without let or hindrance. May it also assist you to enjoy birds as much as Ian and I do.

Peter Scott

Introduction

This book began 37 years ago, for that is how long I have been watching birds. Family lore has it that my interest in them sprang from an intent to sidestep from the long, characteristically uphill walks to which my father was prone on holidays; but certainly I can hardly remember times when birds, my joyful relationship with them and the various other interests that their pursuit has occasioned in my life, did not feature high among my most needed personal fulfilments.

It is difficult for me to analyse precisely why my boyish hobby has become an adult passion, but I no longer question that it will abide. Some of the reasons are very clear. Birds not only fly but also do so in such a range of differing accomplishments that I still feel regular astonishment and untempered envy. Birds are beautiful with a marvellous diversity of form and behaviour, with even the nastiest looking possessing some redeeming aesthetic feature. Birds are freer than I am, not from the event cycles and disciplines of the natural world but certainly from the increasing complex controls of our constructed human society. Envy again? Birds have miraculous powers of survival with, for example, innate navigation systems within them that render our silicone chips no great discovery at all. Birds become real friends, not just as the odd tame individual looking through the window but as calendar witnesses to the turning of the year. Above all, birds provide (within our own) another world to experience and almost share. And birdwatching provides a ready passport to it. Just look out of a window, open the door, and you are there.

Of course there are other natural orders that can provide us with similar experiences or escapes. I regret that the limits of my spare time do not allow me also to enjoy more fully plants, butterflies and small mammals. However, in one hurried life, choices must be made. So I recommend birdwatching as the most easily available alternative to wholly human pursuits. Birds are constantly visible and they are always doing something interesting, if you have or can develop the eye and the wit to perceive it. A birdwatcher may have to face short-term frustrations like rain on binocular lenses, but long-term boredom is never a problem. As the years of study mount up, a deep-seated sense of the avian world's complex rhythms grows, and with it the chance not just to broaden your own understanding but also to contribute directly to the natural history of your home district. This is when the hobby of birdwatching can also become, if you wish, the science of field ornithology, in which Britain and Ireland have a proud record in both amateur and professional fields.

But I am in danger of beginning where I want to end. So let me complete this introduction to the discovery of birds with a simpler explanation of the book. You will find other fuller introductions to birds and birdwatching. This book is not intended to match them. Rather I have hoped to demonstrate within a small space and at a brisk pace the marvels at the end of birdwatching. In the succeeding chapters, you will find first a general statement on birds as a major class of the animal kingdom, together with brief comments on their prehistoric origin, their unique features and the essential discipline of their scientific classification. This is followed by a chapter dealing solely with the fundamental activity of bird observation and identification – finding, seeing, listening, naming – and a discussion of birdwatching both as a pastime and a science, with advice on days in the field and hours of study at home.

At this point the book changes character and becomes an immediate passport to birds and their places. Between March 1978 and January 1979, photographer Philip Sayer and I went to seven famous bird habitats in Scotland and England, and these we have described in some detail. Next comes a month-by-month account of the avian year (or birdwatcher's calendar), and four seasonal extracts from my own log to show just how exciting some birdwatching days can be.

My chief hope for this book is not that it will serve you better than the other guides currently on bookshop shelves. It is that you will find in it a fuller glimpse of the personal fulfilment that surely awaits you in birdwatching. So may it speed your approach to birds out and in of doors, and may you have as many exciting days with them as I have had!

Shovelers

Yellow Wagtail

Little Stint

Birds

At first glance birds appear to form a unique class of animal simply because they fly. Take a longer look round, however, and you will see that their ability to use airspace at will is approached, matched, and even excelled by several other groups of animals, most obviously in the case of bats and hoverflies. The feature that really sets birds apart in their natural class *Aves* is their plumage of feathers. This unique natural clothing is not just for flying; it also helps to conserve the energy required to power flight. Indeed the powerful metabolism of birds makes ours and that of most large mammals seem unremarkable, and has allowed some birds to become the greatest of all animal travellers.

Our understanding of how birds evolved is incomplete. Traditionally it starts from one of the most famous fossil species in science. This was the essentially reptilian yet undoubtedly feathered *Archaeopteryx*. This toothed animal was clearly established in the Jurassic period of the Mesozoic epoch which ended about 135 million years ago. Although

Gannets: primitive but specialist fish-eaters, related to pelicans.

probably incapable of full flight, it provides a clear link between its own reptilian or small dinosaurial ancestors and the first examples of true untoothed birds that appeared among the fossil fauna of the Cretaceous period in both North and South America and Europe. The latter include forms that structurally resemble groups of birds still in existence, such as cormorants and geese.

In the more extensive display of fossils of the Tertiary epoch, the increasing diversification of avian types is obvious and groups which we would immediately recognize today as hawks, game and wading birds occurred throughout the Eocene period, which ended 40 million years ago. Indeed, it is probable that most existing groups of larger birds were established by then. Unfortunately the accidents of fossilization do not seem to have affected many smaller birds. Their prehistoric identification begins in the Oligocene period, about 30 million years ago, but they are generally assumed to be of relatively recent development. Their diversification was much affected by the vicissitudes of the Ice Ages, which clearly disrupted patterns of distribution.

Continuing evolution is made apparent by the variation of both structure and plumage colours shown by populations at the end of a species' range or those that have become isolated. Within the total range of many species, these variations may be sufficient to warrant the splitting into subspecies. These may be regarded as the final signpost of evolution in a species before the completed process of natural selection leads on to another closely related but genetically separate species. In history, birds are much older than Man – who has been enviously watching them fly away for only 3 million years. Sparrows have long existed without houses!

While birds are not unique in their powers of flight, they have become more wholly adapted to the retention and development of flight than any other animal class. Their employment of flight in relation to both their general life style and individual behaviour is markedly uniform. True some birds, such as the Ostrich and the Kiwi, have found (or rediscovered) a mode of life that has allowed them to give up flight; but in the main, the dramatically advantageous use of airspace by birds has been sustained only by a continuous and high degree of specialization in limb use, bone structure and musculature. The chief character of this has been the development of forelimbs into wings of common structure but different outlines and efficiencies, determined by individual needs in short or long range movement and manoeuvrability.

In all flying birds, the wings are powered by large breast muscles attached to a deep keel on the central chest bone. To improve the output of flight power in relation to total weight, the externally visible changes to structure have been asso-

swallow

gull

ciated with internal alterations to bone formation, tension and attitude. Unlike those of mammals, bird skeletons contain many bones that are hollow and have air in sacs. These, together with those areas of the plumage that are effectively mechanical in action (the longest wing and all tail feathers) and the streamlining of head and body, form the most highly evolved adaptation to sustained flight in the higher animal kingdom. We have tried to copy it, but even our most advanced inventions in sailing or powered flight remain inflexible and inefficient by comparison. Watch any slow motion film of a flying bird for evidence of this.

In addition to the wing and tail feathers that as aerofoils create lift into and sustain movement through the air, birds also require feathers to protect their thin-skinned bodies and to regulate their highly efficient metabolism or power source.

Like mammals and ourselves, birds have achieved the superior and less fickle energy flow of hot blood; and almost all remain fully active throughout even the coldest winters. Thus birds have many more feathers than just those that form their visible outer plumage. Effectively they live within what we used to call eiderdowns but now name duvets. When it is exceptionally cold and wet, birds can expand these downy layers and reduce their losses of heat and energy. However at all times birds are, in terms of bone and muscle, much smaller than the mass of their plumage suggests. To understand this and to see the complexity of feathering, ask your nearest pigeon fancier to let you handle one of his birds, or watch your butcher pluck a chicken.

The giving up of their forelimbs to the effort and advantage of flight has meant that birds have become two-legged. Apart from those groups that are almost exclusively aerial (and feed in flight, like swallows), or are aquatic (and feed on or under water, like penguins), and so use ground locomotion only in a restricted nesting space, birds move over most terrains with considerable skill and often delicate balance. Their legs and feet are set below the equilibrium of their bodies and flex through wide angles at both the knee (usually hidden by the body plumage), the ankle (or tarsal joint, appearing to be a reversed knee), and the toes. As with wings, the relative lengths of these parts vary according to the dictates of each bird's preferred environment and way of life; but moving over the ground all birds either walk or hop, these two basic progressions being developed respectively into running or climbing. Small birds that habitually perch have also developed a self-locking system of tendons that allow their feet a secure grip on the slimmest twig or wire.

Even more striking than the various adapted locomotions of birds are the multiple use that birds have made of what for them must replace the feeding apparatus of other animals. In place of lips and teeth freely assisted by paws and hands, birds use only beak or bill partially assisted by feet and toe claws. Accordingly, evolution has caused many variations in beak, bill and feet structure, and these form one of the basic and most visible keys to their classification. They indicate to us not only different groups of birds but even the individual habits which are necessary to prevent wasteful competition in the finding and eating of food.

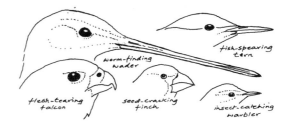

There are of course many other features about birds that merit discussion; of these, the fact that the most specialized flying class in all creation still adopts the basic and vulnerable breeding behaviour of their reptilian ancestors (laying eggs in nests) stands out in distinct contrast to their achievement along with mammals and ourselves of hot blood. Clearly in evolutionary terms, changes in their reproductive system have offered birds less overall advantage than the others already discussed. In particular the classic advantage of flight would be seriously diminished by any development of weighty embryos. Such extra loading could ground any small bird and all would have to accept slower take-offs and an increased risk of predation. Natural selection has avoided such a nonsense.

However it is not the purpose of this book to answer every question in avian biology. What I wish to stress is the unique success of birds as flying animals. To this end, it is worth recalling the other tribe of flying or gliding animals also first known from the fossil record of the Jurassic period. This was the group of goblin-like creatures called pterodactyls, which successfully developed certain bird-like structures. They had light wing bones, but supporting flaps of thin skin, not feathers. Pterodactyls became common in the Cretaceous period but by its end, about 63 million years ago, they and the ground dinosaurs had become extinct. So it seems that the development of feathered plumage was the crux of avian success and that it has led to the evolution of a major animal class that has stood all the tests and trials of our planet for over 100 million years.

Plumage, as I have already explained, performs two major functions and it is likely that it is the less obvious of these – the energy conserving mechanism – that has conferred the most lasting benefit in evolutionary terms. To fly was not enough, to fly efficiently was. With this skill came the means also to maintain high levels of activity in a wide range of habitats and climates. Small wonder then that in terms of diversity, birds far outnumber mammals and all other vertebrate animals except fishes, and have been able to reach and breed in every part of the world except the polar ice caps and the very highest mountain peaks.

At the peak of avian diversity, during the Pliocene period between 13 and 2 million years ago, there were probably 11,600 species. Later the cycles of glaciation that characterized the Pleistocene period, and ceased only 10,000 years ago, brought extreme and abrupt pressures of climate and habitat change. These totally disrupted the ecology of many species and it is estimated that 3,000 died out; of these, 800 can be identified in the fossil record but the remaining 2,200 have been entirely lost. However the pattern of distribution of the remaining 8,600 suggests that those lost were mainly higher latitude species, which were unable to develop migratory (withdrawal) behaviour quickly enough to avoid the periods of extreme cold or heat.

Nowadays the richest avifauna in the world exists in tropical South America. Indeed the Neotropical region as a whole easily leads the rest of the world in its diversity of both avian families and species. This region of lengthy geographical isolation has also many primitive species (including the Hoatzin which as a nestling retains the ability to use its vestigial wingclaws for climbing), and the high number of

31

wholly indigenous families out of a regional total of 86.

After the Neotropical region, the richest areas for birds are, in descending order, the partially linked Ethiopian (Africa) and Oriental (India and South-east Asia); the closely linked Nearctic (North America) and Palaearctic (Eurasia); and the again long isolated and, significantly, most oceanic, Australian. The Nearctic and Palaearctic are often combined in zoogeographical terms in the Holarctic region (Northern Hemisphere except the subtropical and tropical belts). No less than 48 of the 83 avian families to be found within the Holarctic occur on both its major land masses, and the whole avifauna is dominated by highly migratory species adapted to exploit the sudden insect and seed crops of the northern summer. Britain is on the western edge of Eurasia, and so it is the birds of the Western Palaearctic that you will be watching. Later on I will explain how you can hope to see the odd one from the Nearctic, too.

Before ending this chapter on birds, I must explain one thing more. This is your need at the outset to come to grips with some of the scientific vocabulary of bird study, as a means of solving a few of the puzzles that will arise. I can illustrate this best by ending with some words on the subject of scientific classification or, in one word, systematics. Already I have had to use words like "class" and "species" freely, and without a fuller understanding of these (and a

dictionary close by) you will find the business of bird identification can be very confusing. In arriving at a precise position or name for each kind of bird or its geographical form, ornithologists (professional and expert amateur bird-watchers) have, as other scientists, adopted a method of eight-stage classification and a standard set of Latin names that override the vagaries of vernacular language. Taking as an example the House Sparrow of Britain, its classification is:

I	Kingdom	Animal, not plant
II	Branch	Vertebrate *Vertebrata*, possessing a backbone
III	Class	Birds *Aves*, possessing feathered plumage
IV	Order	Perching birds *Passeriformes*, mostly composed of song birds *Oscines*
V	Family	Weavers *Ploceidae*, mostly small finch-like birds of social behaviour and of Ethiopian origin but with representatives throughout temperate Palaearctic
VI	Genus	Sparrow *Passer*, small weavers with structure, plumage and behaviour distinct from other genera in family

| VII | Species | House Sparrow *Passer domesticus*, sparrow genetically separated from nearest relative Spanish Sparrow *Passer Hispaniolensis* and living in closer association with Man *Homo Sapiens* than any other bird |
| VIII | Subspecies | (Northern) House Sparrow *Passer domesticus domesticus*, nominate or first named form with some plumage characters significantly different from those of other forms. resident around Mediterranean Sea and elsewhere |

The above may strike you as a very long-winded way of defining a sparrow, but such disciplines are crucial to any developed enjoyment of birds. Furthermore if you look closely at it, you may spot what I hope will be the first of the many surprises and springs of intense interest in this book. Your local sparrows are not really typical birds of Britain, being in fact long established immigrants from Africa, the ancestral home of all weavers. So suddenly the world is smaller, and my first chapter finished.

16

Observation and Identification

Finding

In looking for and finding birds, you should recognize first that you are hunting; without doubt the successful observer of nature is essentially undertaking a more ancient pursuit. So even if, happily, it does not end in the death of a selected prey, it is worth real commitment and an understanding of the various fieldcrafts involved. These develop best through repeated trial and error, but there are some simple rules that bear declaration. Not all the birds that you will wish to study will occur in your garden and street, or stay close as readily as the ducks and seagulls in your local park. So learning where and how to approach your bird quarry will save you many if not all misses. Where to find them is dealt with in the chapter on bird habitats; here we are concerned with how to search for them once you are there.

The first rule is to be quiet, always. Although birds have no visible ear their hearing is extremely acute, and through use of it many escape the eyes of even the most expert watcher. So watch your step; learn to read the ground ahead, particularly for pitfalls, dry branches, and loose stones. Head up and eyes forward may spot you an interesting bird, but the snap of an unseen and carelessly trodden twig could lose it in the next moment. Do not wear squeaking clothes or clanking equipment, and above all, don't talk loudly or shout "There it is!" Penetrating whispers are the communications order of most days. The rule of quietness applies at all times, even when you are actively searching over a wide horizon. It is most crucial during the final stalk after the one bird that you want to observe closely.

Allied to the rule of quietness is the rule of careful movement. You need not always walk slowly but try to keep your advance easy and regular, avoiding sudden changes in pace and direction. Running is not advisable, though there are occasions (like following a hawk which dashes behind a slope) when it is difficult to resist. Be careful, too, when you stop to watch the birds ahead or wait for them to re-appear. This is the rule of patience. Eventually most birds will accept a kindly human presence, but a sudden change in attitude or an expression of exasperation may drive the one that you are after back into cover, just as it was about to come out. So sit down and rise up slowly, have your binoculars ready (around your neck, never in their case), and don't have to wrestle for your notebook or a passing-time cigarette. Changing your vantage point may pay off but try to make your first choice the right one. There is a hidden advantage in the rules of patience and preparation; you will frequently see birds that you did not expect. It is true that Kingfishers will perch on fishing rods held by still fishermen.

Another important rule is to make the greatest possible use of cover and the lie of the land. Avoid walking along or stand-

ing about on skylines at all costs. Do not run across gaps in hedges; or trample through low vegetation; firstly because your bird may be in it, and secondly because there is often a break in even the thickest bramble patch if you look closely enough. So use "dead ground", like folds in fields; keep behind the screens of hedges; walk around thickets; move through or stand in shadows; sit near or in bushes, not in the open. In short, make yourself as invisible as possible. If this is impractical (on moor or mudflat, for example), remember again the rules of quietness and relative stillness. Crouching sometimes helps, but it makes for your own discomfort ere long. Straightening up to ease your thigh muscles near birds will cost you more than slowly stalking them in a constant posture.

Another rule concerns camouflage. Wear sombre clothing; lurid anoraks and fluorescent gumboots are out. Dress instead in greys, olives, browns or blacks, so that you will merge into the background of the habitat as much as possible. Make certain that your clothing and footwear are comfortable, both for moving and staying still. A dose of tight jeans plus knee cramp may be ungovernable just as the bird appears. Throughout your searches, try to put yourself in the bird's position; imagine its view of you and the background cover or land and work out the line of approach closest to invisibility or least obviousness. Remember always that a little more care

Fieldcraft example: observer half-hidden by pine sprays, watching passerine migrants in coastal cover.

or a slightly wider circle will pay extra dividends in close observation.

The final rule is that of concentration and there are two stages to it. When you are searching for birds, you will need to develop virtually all-round vision by using not just the acuity of your eye's centre but also the sensitivity to movement of its outer surround. You must make constant judgements about the likely places within the habitat that will hold the most birds. You must spot behaviour that tells of disturbance (time for you to stand still). You must learn, for example, that birds usually take off into wind, that those that eat insects like sunny lees or the interface of sun and shadow within a wood, and that all usually return to a preferred niche – often the one from which you first disturb them. So initially your concentration has to be general. However the moment that you are after one individual bird, it must be singular. Put aside the temptations of others even if they pop out in front of you, and just think about the one bird. Does it look settled? Is it feeding happily? Put yourself again in its place, try and forecast its next move and behaviour. This is the time for total concentration on one other living being and remembering the earlier rules. The final approach, however nerve tingling, must be calm, and absolute care is necessary if it is not to end in a burst of wingbeats and a muffled curse.

If all this seems rather rigorous, don't worry. Practice will help and soon you will be observing at least some of the rules automatically.

Before leaving the subject of finding birds, I must warn you that the successful birdwatcher is an early riser. Except when extreme weather or the tasks of breeding alters their behaviour and makes, for example, feeding an all day trial for them, few birds are constantly visible in their preferred habitat. Accordingly, if you leave your start in observation until mid-morning, you will have missed the best of a birdwatcher's day; and if you go home well before dusk, you will not observe the often busy end to a bird's day. These statements are particularly true of the small perching birds, but as a general rule, I advise packing as much observation as possible into the first three and last two hours of the day. You can afford a snooze in the early afternoon, especially on hot days, but on no account lie in bed wondering what you will see. Get up and see it.

Another natural rhythm that requires your attention is the timing of the sea's tide. On your visits to coasts and estuaries, "getting the tide wrong" can be terribly frustrating. A line of dots far out on a vast mudflat is likely to defeat the largest telescope; surf roaring over the top sands of a beach will have already sent many species to distant roosts. If you have plenty of time, I recommend the full observation of an incoming tide; if not, try and catch the last hour and a half before full tide.

Tide tables are usually available at the local anglers' shop; daily tide times also often feature in local papers.

For those of you beginning to wilt under the above disciplines (or just the thought of them), there is an alternative strategy. It is best summed up as "wait and see". Traditionally this passive and therefore more restful method of observing birds has been conducted from hides, essentially wooden or canvas boxes from which you peep out on birds that are unaware of your existence. I have to admit to preferring stalking to watching from hides, but the latter has produced some marvellous moments with such shy species as wild geese and small crakes. In recent years, the "wait and see" tactic has been widely used in the monitoring of seabird distribution and movements, and of visible migration along coasts and over land. With its use you can often combine with birdwatching the ultimate in passive pursuits, just sitting in the sun. You will find further comment on this type of birdwatching in my descriptions of Flamborough Head and North Norfolk.

There are more developed forms of bird hunting, such as trapping for close examination, and ringing and the accurate annual counting of populations, but these require fairly advanced skills and even more disciplines. Furthermore they are only practised with the permission of, or with advice from, the British Trust for Ornithology, and are best seen

Near Blythburgh, Suffolk; southern estuary with high-tide perches for kingfishers and invertebrate-rich mud for wading birds.

as developments in your hobby rather than initial aims.

Finally, while the finding of birds does allow you the freedom and excitement of a skilful chase, you are legally bound not to wilfully disturb them in any way. Particularly when you are faced with a shy and very probably exhausted vagrant, you may have to leave it in peace without fully naming it. Never mind, there will be others.

Seeing

You have successfully stalked or waited on a particular bird or flock, but can you really see it? This is an important question and the answer will determine your real success or failure as an observer. For example, there is no point at all in looking at your quarry if the sun or strong light is behind it. It will be a mere silhouette, and even size and structure will be hard to judge. So the first rule of seeing is not to be content with a quiet and cautious approach, but to be instantly ready to begin detailed observation; you have to think about seeing at the end of finding, and learn to make the best judgement of when to switch activities. You must pay particular attention to keeping the light source behind or to one side of you, to making sure that you do not flush other birds or a mammal at the last moment (and so scare everything off), and to constantly assessing the best range for observation related both to your own eye power (in case the bird moves quickly)

and to your binocular power (in case you are still too far for detailed plumage observation). Having your quarry in good even light can be worth several score yards of closer range, and physical comfort is essential to real concentration.

The second rule in seeing is to look at your bird methodically. This is important particularly as a basis for naming and noting behaviour, though I am not saying that you cannot just enjoy the aesthetic appearance of birds as well. At all times your binoculars should be not only round your neck but with their lenses clean and properly adjusted. Imprecise focussing and a prism out of alignment will only cause your eyes to suffer from what my wife calls "fruit machine action", and they may take long moments to recover from it. Your notebook and field guide should be handy in easy opening pockets, and your pencil sharp and not lost. These items checked, and with any panting caused by a final crawl in control, you can raise your binoculars, steady them (if possible, with elbow against a bank or on a knee), and look at the bird. Incidentally, many people take some time to get used to locating subjects in the field of view of binoculars, so it is well worth practising on other less flighty things than birds. Always try to place the additional optical power directly along the established cone of vision between your eyes and the bird. Never jam the lenses into your eyes and cast about!

In most cases, your first reaction at the sight of an enlarged bird or birds will be aesthetic. Suddenly they are more beautiful than you thought. Certainly the difference in their carriage and movement from mammals always thrills me. However almost immediately a name will flash into your brain. At first, it will probably be a group or generic one – swan, thrush, seagull – but as your skill at seeing and your knowledge of naming grow, it will be specific – Mute Swan, Song Thrush, Blackheaded Gull. The process of identification is discussed in the next section and is obviously fundamental for any fuller study of the quarry. Without it, what you see and may enjoy will be left in scientific suspense. But don't worry, I suffer from this even after 37 years.

As you go on watching, the immediate activity of the bird or birds will gain substance in your mind. You will begin to perceive it more fully as a unique animal, even a being. To allow such perception of its life and character to be free of any human bias, another rule is essential. Do not cloud its singular ability to create wonder. You are seeing the finite miracle of an evolution quite separate to yours, and what it does may well be more interesting than what you think it is or ought to be doing. The White Stork does not bring babies but (happily for many African farmers) it can spot a locust through 20 yards of grass. That is the skill in which you should vicariously revel. Indeed not to watch birds or any

other natural class of animal in full innocence is to prejudice your perception of life's total variety and essential order. So seeing must contain both accurate inspection and unadulterated reception. Only after such process is complete should your imagination be employed to set and sort out the puzzles.

As you become experienced in seeing, some things will be for ever obvious and easy to remember – for example the way an aggressive cock Blackbird cocks its tail right up on landing – but many more will be hard to encompass in your mind, let alone remember precisely. Every lazy, notebook-less observer finds this out to his or her cost. So another basic rule of seeing is not to trust your memory. Even the simplest notes can create a fund of knowledge, and as a disciplined observer you have a real opportunity to add to science. And even if that seems a bit ambitious at this stage, don't ignore the lasting pleasure of your personal records. Start them now.

When the bird is a new one to you, you will find it essential to write a description on the spot. Of course, you may find it immediately in your field guide but even if you do, try and digest your own reaction to it and annotate the text or illustration.

All observers do not see birds the same way; some eyes are more drawn to colour, others to form or character; others still may be weak in judging structure. So you must learn the filters to your own perception early. When you know the bird but it does something odd, describe the action or behaviour factually before adding any interpretation. If you are counting the birds of a particular community or area, put the numbers down as they come.

Lastly, a point on how to count. Individual numbering is the most accurate method, but it is often impossible – for instance, with a dense flock of Starlings or a pack of fast flying duck. Thus most birdwatchers count in multiple units. I use 3's, 10's and even 100's on occasion and you will find such units quite practical, once your eye and mind are used to the task. Just remember to run the odd check on the multiple unit method by also occasionally counting the same flock by individual numbering. Most people underestimate when counting in units.

Listening

Although your eyes are the organs most important to your birdwatching success, your ears come close to them in usefulness. Bird voices vary just as much as bird characters and plumages, and on many occasions you will hear your quarry before you see it. There will be other times when being sure of a small difference of tone or phrase may be the final clue in the naming process. Furthermore if you are out at night after owls, tracing the source of a hoot or screech is the only way to have any chance of seeing the flitting ghost that utters them. So throughout your search of habitats, your approach to individual birds or flocks and your observation of them, open ears will be as useful to you as skinned eyes.

Since hearing varies as much as vision in human beings and the transcription of avian sound is more difficult than the description of plumage, it is important to assess your own powers and range of reception carefully. I suffer from a dominant right ear and frequently have to ask companions for a corrected direction. So make sure where your ears hear, and that you can relate the forms in which you receive calls or songs to those generally transcribed in the literature. The simplest way to do these checks is to go out with a practised birdwatcher and get him or her to monitor your reception.

Listening is a particularly important form of search in

dense cover, where your sight of birds may well be only a series of tantalizing glimpses. It can also provide clues to the whereabouts of birds moving ahead of you, to those passing overhead in nocturnal migration, and even to the identity of those dots on that vast mudflat mentioned earlier. Again bird calls and songs are best learnt through trial and error, but you may feel it worthwhile to invest in one or two of the excellent records now available.

Naming

You have made a careful and close approach; you have your quarry in full view, and have seen it well. However you cannot name it precisely. You can think of many birds that it is *not* but its specific identity escapes you. How do you capture it?

I have already demonstrated, in the first chapter, the way in which all creatures are classified. We owe this systematic approach mostly to a Swedish naturalist, Linnaeus, who towards the end of the eighteenth century first established the disciplines of individual identities and relationships in the natural world by the introduction of Latin nomenclature. The legacy of his sequential separation of species and the clarity of his approach remain the basis of all later observational science. Any attempt at bird identification that lacks or obscures by specious short cuts the recognition of the basic tree of relationship, spreading out from the branches

Interface of wood and marsh, Tresco, providing sunny lee, different plants, and hence many seeds and insects. 62 passerine species have been seen from this spot.

25

of orders and families to the twigs and twiglets of genera and species, leads to dangerous confusion. Sadly, some bird books with tempting glossy pictures fall into this trap. So before you spend much time in the field, I advise you to survey the whole avifauna that occurs in Western Europe and add to your established recognition of the more obvious bird families that live around you – for instance, sparrows, starlings, tits, thrushes and crows – some prior experience of the less obvious ones that you may not have seen as being different or have been hiding in the nearest wood and farmland. Examples of these are finches, warblers, plovers and partridges.

The easiest way to make such a survey is to read and digest one of the marvellously illustrated modern summaries of the avian world. These are written in systematic order and contain the essential physical and behavioural characters of each order and family. The one that I recommend is *The Dictionary of Birds in Colour* by Bruce Campbell, which contains an excellent selection of colour photographs. Having digested that, you are ready for a visit to a museum of natural history or, preferably, a zoo. For reasons of some strange purism that escape me, many current birdwatchers tend to look down their noses at the study of stuffed or captive birds, but for the beginner it represents another easily tapped source of early knowledge. So I suggest

frequent visits to the ornithological collection in your nearest zoo or stately home. I don't agree with the basic principle of confinement, but I do enjoy the proximity with birds that this allows. In fact I still love "feeding the ducks".

To start you off, the chart of bird relationships that follows will give you a grasp of the avian tree. This will save you many mistakes and allow you to build up your skill in bird identification much more securely than staggering half blind through the small print of a field guide, of which even the best contains dangerously compressed facts and imperfect plates.

Sometimes bird identification appears impossible – alas, our eyes will never be as keen as those of a Kestrel – but every bird species has at least one unique (or diagnostic) character; which is why your homework is so important. If this is not readily visible in its plumage, then it will be somewhere in its vocabulary or behaviour, and it is such that field ornithologists and museum workers have sought and are still seeking to isolate. The process of observation and definition can be long and hard. Experts disagree on bird identification as they do on most other subjects. However the challenge is tremendously exciting and open to all; and the satisfaction is immense when you suddenly see in the bird not just a general relationship but its absolute and specific identity. Few tests of observation effect a more pleasurable involvement of

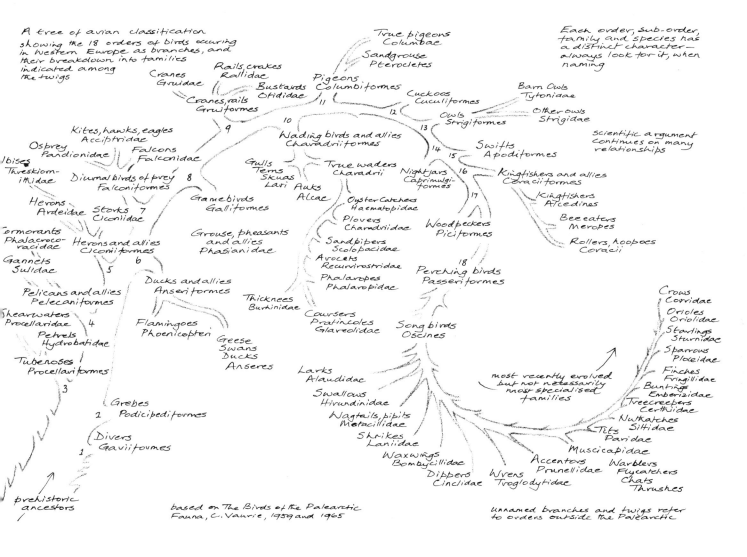

A tree of avian classification showing the 18 orders of birds occurring in Western Europe as branches, and their breakdown into families indicated among the twigs

Each order, sub-order, family and species has a distinct character— always look for it, when naming

True pigeons
Columbae

Sandgrouse
Pterocletes

Pigeons
Columbiformes

Cranes
Gruidae

Rails, crakes
Rallidae

Bustards
Otididae

Cuckoos
Cuculiformes

Barn Owls
Tytonidae

Cranes, rails
Gruiformes

Owls
Strigiformes

Other owls
Strigidae

Kites, hawks, eagles
Accipitridae

Wading birds and allies
Charadriiformes

Swifts
Apodiformes

scientific argument continues on many relationships

Osprey
Pandionidae

Falcons
Falconidae

Ibises
Threskiornithidae

Gulls
Terns
Skuas
Lari

True waders
Charadrii

Nightjars
Caprimulgiformes

Kingfishers and allies
Coraciiformes

Diurnal birds of prey
Falconiformes

Auks
Alcae

Kingfishers
Alcedines

Herons
Ardeidae

Storks
Ciconiidae

Gamebirds
Galliformes

Oyster Catchers
Haematopidae

Woodpeckers
Piciformes

Bee eaters
Merops

Cormorants
Phalacrocoracidae

Herons and allies
Ciconiiformes

Plovers
Charadriidae

Rollers, hoopoes
Coracii

Gannets
Sulidae

Grouse, pheasants and allies
Phasianidae

Sandpipers
Scolopacidae

Avocets
Recurvirostridae

Perching birds
Passeriformes

Pelicans and allies
Pelecaniformes

Ducks and allies
Anseriformes

Thicknees
Burtinidae

Phalaropes
Phalaropidae

Crows
Corvidae

Shearwaters
Procellariidae

Petrels
Hydrobatidae

Flamingoes
Phoenicopteri

Geese
Swans
Ducks
Anseres

Coursers
Pratincoles
Glareolidae

Songbirds
Oscines

Orioles
Oriolidae

Starlings
Sturnidae

Tubenoses
Procellariiformes

Larks
Alaudidae

Sparrows
Ploceidae

Finches
Fringillidae

Grebes
Podicipediformes

Swallows
Hirundinidae

most recently evolved but not necessarily most specialised families

Buntings
Emberizidae

Treecreepers
Certhiidae

Divers
Gaviiformes

Wagtails, pipits
Motacillidae

Shrikes
Laniidae

Nuthatches
Sittidae

Tits
Paridae

Waxwings
Bombycillidae

Muscicapidae

prehistoric
ancestors

Dippers
Cinclidae

Wrens
Troglodytidae

Accentors
Prunellidae

Warblers
Flycatchers
Chats
Thrushes

based on The Birds of the Palearctic Fauna, C. Vaurie, 1959 and 1965

unnamed branches and twigs refer to orders outside the Palearctic

memory, sight and mental argument than bird identification. So it really is worth preparing for it; when the subject is a rare shearwater going by at 20 knots a mile offshore, your inner debate has to be fast and clinical!

Next you must take account of the fact that the appearance of birds will be neither constant nor necessarily complete. They do not always fit their book description; this is not just because of varying distances or differing light factors but because key characters may be absent or only show in certain circumstances. A bird's appearance can alter with

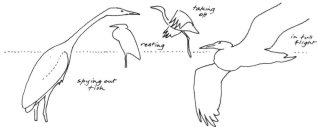

changes in stance and action. Thus herons look incredibly long necked and slim chested when just about to spear a fish, but are seemingly troubled with goitre in flight when their aerial equilibrium demands neck retraction. Again many species pass through various and at times bewildering stages of plumage, according to season or age. Robins just out of nest have no red breast but lots of spots which indicate

their affinity to thrushes. So understand that most birds will not stand in front of you and precisely match the illustrations of the adult male in your guide. You must therefore beware of this and other vagaries, such as moult, plumage wear and albinism (changing feather colours), and seek to establish the multiple image that each species forms in the expert eye.

The best way to raise your guard to confusing images is to get to know one species really well. I suggest the Starling, which can walk, hop and run, look fat or sleek, and of which distant flocks can appear to resemble thrushes or waders. Learn how to encompass the multiple image of one species and you are well on the way to seeing those of the rest. Bird identification is not easy and, as I have just indicated, there are as many pitfalls with common species as there are with great rarities.

Now back to the bird in front of you. It is not like any other that you have seen and named and, unless you are very unlike me, your heart is thumping loudly at the prospect of identifying a new bird species. You have thumbed through your field guide but not found it. So there is no easy answer to the question. The next rule to be applied is fundamental. It is to construct a positive identification of the species and to avoid at all costs a merely negative elimination of all others. In reaching this goal, your four most important tools are prior knowledge, the ability to see and hear, the requisites to write a description and make sketches (however rough), and the chance of careful research or expert discussion later on.

For a start, forget about the last; what or who may help in due course is not important at this stage. Time is pressing; the bird may fly. Begin therefore with the most basic facts and build your record from there. It is unlikely that your start point will just be "bird" for, as I have already indicated, you should have enabled yourself to get closer to sorting out bird families, even if your start is approximate. Thus your description may begin with "small perching bird, recalling Robin in stance and action", or "duck, more compact than Mallard, constantly diving". Such first words as these are much better (and more scientific) attempts at naming than the facile choice of just the closest image out of many similar ones on a crowded plate. In fact the two quotations above immediately suggest to me that the small bird was a chat such

The multiple image of the Starling

10 different silhouettes, all made by the same species

as Redstart, and that the duck was a diving species and not a surface-feeding species like Mallard.

Having fixed the bird's basic type, your notes should be expanded as quickly and as far as possible. I find it useful to note next the characters that most catch my eye – for example, "wags tail", "wholly black plumage", "very buoyant flight", "long pink legs", or "striking white bar across wings" – and I always try for a general summary of the bird before starting to define the finer points of plumage or behaviour, such as "thin whitish ring round eye", "underwing dark grey", or "walks but also breaks into loping run". It is helpful, again by way of discipline, to note the latter details in a set order against a mental map of the bird's plumage or standard list of character terms and actions. To illustrate this, I have laid out an actual description and added to it the sort of analysis needed to convert a sighting to a positively established identification. If possible, you should undertake the latter process immediately so that time for checking details on the actual bird is available. However this may be impossible, and a major reason for disciplined notetaking is to provide a lasting record which you can study away from the heat of the moment and with a steadier heart. Do not expect success every time. It is always exasperating when one has to scrap or change an identification, but even the most expert birdwatchers that I know have to do so on occasion. So don't fear

mistakes; they will teach you much more than lucky first judgements or the slavish ticking off of birds that others name.

Your greatest resource in bird identification is your personal experience and knowledge, which should be carefully banked in notebook and log. They frequently develop into a real talent and once you have that, then the worst (or best) challenges of bird identification, for example separating Marsh Warblers from Reed Warblers, will not be beyond you. Even today you could be the first to crack such a problem. There are plenty of teasers left in bird identification!

As you move into birdwatching circles, do not be shy of asking for help and advice from your companions. Amateur birdwatchers have a proud record for passing on the basic skills of their hobby. Just take care to pick on the one who works his notebook hard and is using essentially scientific disciplines to add to his or her enjoyment. He will be a better teacher than the others glibly shouting out names or twitching excitedly on the nearest skyline.

small gull

passing N at c. 60 yards, with Kittiwakes (adult and immature)

Seen thro' 10 x 40 binocs. during seawatch

1st thought - imm. Kittiwake but bird smaller and slighter, with deeper, more fluid wing-beats and more "buoyancy" - eye caught by "hood", white neck collar, jet black outer-wing, contrasting with brownish-grey coverts and very white secondaries

half-hood sharply cut off, forming white collar - very striking

"jet black" area, making outer wing look long/ sharp

clear white, not sullied as in imm. kittiwake

Flamborough Head
0626 hrs. 7-5.79

Light bright, under broken clouds, fog-bank to N; wind SW force 2-3; slight frost

no other observers present

many Gannets moving N - Little Auk on 6-5

forked, with obvious black rim

Size of. kittiwake

"10%" shorter in wing length

dull band on greater coverts

small bill

white tips (in guide) did not show but feathers looked sharp-pointed

no colour seen

body bulkier

wing-coverts, mantle grey, but with brownish tone and uniform

→ "10-15%" shorter in body length

obviously not Kittiwake
- too small, wing-pattern different (no "zig-zag")
- forked tail and hood
= Sabine's Gull

colour of wing-coverts and mantle points to 1st summer bird, as does incomplete hood

imm. Kittiwake (seen 5 mins. later)

black "zig-zag" still obvious

* specific identification and ageing checked against Handbook and found correct 0920, same day

inner primaries marked with dusky

31

Bird Studies and Equipment

The last chapter has given you guidance on the fundamental skills of observation and identification. Now we come to their deployment into the major activities in birdwatching, and some advice about equipment and fuller involvement with other birdwatchers.

It is a good idea early on to make at least one exploratory study of a particular place and the birds that it sustains throughout the year. Not to have your own study area is to miss both the most thought provoking contact and the most intimate experience possible with birds. In these days of frenetic automobility, many birdwatchers seem content just to dash off after the next rare bird; but that particular form of birdwatching, accurately described as "twitching", has long since proved too sterile for me, and for many other observers that I admire. Too much collection, far too little understanding. So I advise against it as a major activity though it is difficult to resist completely (and the occasional burst can be very exciting, if the bird is still there). Over the years, I have made prolonged and often solitary studies of ten habitats as various as a foreshore in southern Scotland and a soda lake in Kenya. Currently, I am a member of a small group trying to define the avian year of a Humberside headland more fully than ever before; it is from this kind of exploration that my experienced rather than learned knowledge of birds has come.

The choice of a study area is not difficult. It starts with the purchase of the relevant 1″ Ordnance Survey map, and the search thereon for a discrete habitat or prominent feature of the landscape that you can visit regularly without too much expense. It could be a length of a disused railway track or a river, your nearest reservoir, a common with scrub and some pools; anywhere in fact where disturbance is low and you can find and count the birds. Having made your choice, go and spend a few hours in it and let the birds do the rest. It will be surprising if they don't immediately capture your interest, and you can quickly distil that into the field notes, counts, rough maps, and habitat descriptions that together form the basis of a lasting appreciation of the place's ornithology. It is advisable to start with a small study area of under 200 acres and not too many types of habitat; your nearest park or common may be the best place for you, but don't let me put off a wider adventure if you feel bold. You will see in the section on Regent's Park that my most enjoyable study encompassed 600 acres.

As the study of your own place and its birds lengthens, you will probably find that certain aspects of bird behaviour will tug at your mind and heart more than others. For me it has always been the miracle of migration that heightens the expectations of every spring and autumn day. The study of that phenomenon has also taken me to many bird observa-

Migrant cover on England's E. coast, affording instant shelter and food; best searched by paired observers gently pushing birds into wind.

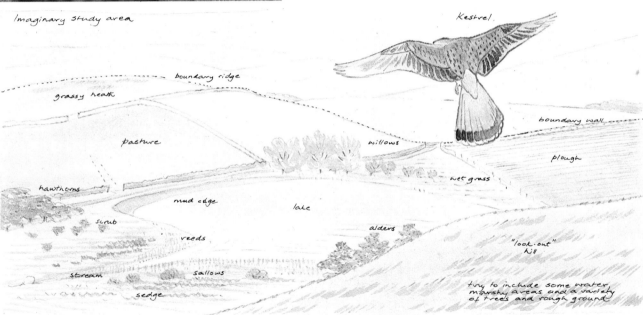

Imaginary study area

Kestrel

boundary ridge

grassy heath

pasture

willows

boundary wall

plough

hawthorns

mud edge

lake

wet grass

scrub

reeds

alders

"look-out" hill

stream

sallows

sedge

try to include some water, marshy areas and a variety of trees and rough ground

33

tories and end points throughout three continents. However I have tried to keep at least one eye open for other things, and I can remember or still notice events in which the bird's behaviour was far removed from long-distance movement; for example, the marvellous "folk dance" performed by Pied Wagtails one Cambridge morning 25 years ago, or the utterly miserable appearance of oiled seabirds on too many recent days by the North Sea. Indeed once you have the basic skills and the experience of regular observation upon one bird community, you will be qualified to start on many pursuits. Some birdwatchers spend their holidays, time and money on the exploration of distant countries whose birds are little known; others devote themselves to one family or even one species; others still to particular studies of general behaviour, and so on. The study fields are immense and in no way is our knowledge of any of them complete. But in making your choice of a more specialized study, be careful not to over-reach yourself.

In Britain, many birdwatchers have in the last 30 years combined into a formidable force of "ringers" and spend most of their time catching, measuring, and ringing birds with tiny light metal bands. The application of ringing to the study of bird populations first stemmed from the wish to define the direction and timing of migration, as shown from the recoveries of ringed birds; but nowadays the technique, allied with statistical analysis, allows the study of survival, population densities, and precise biometrics as well. It has become a very important activity within the total scene of birdwatching and if getting close to birds becomes particularly exciting for you, ringing must appeal. However I must warn you that because of the risks inherent in it (of disturbance and very occasionally actual wounding of birds), you are not free to start tomorrow. You are required to take an apprenticeship alongside a qualified person and to obtain a permit from the British Trust for Ornithology before undertaking any catching or ringing of birds. I am no longer a ringer, being too restless and preferring the challenge of the field to that in the hand; however I do have fond memories of stumbling but successful drives into traps or mist-nets. So by all means try it, but not to the total exclusion of everything else.

In recent years, the more advanced studies of birds have tended to coalesce into what is termed conservation, and they have attracted ecological as well as ornithological disciplines. If birds are really to mean something to you, you must have a proper care for them and understand that their survival may have a direct bearing upon or value for many more people than yourself. This value may be the reverse of your own, but fortunately in Western Europe it is increasingly set high and held in trust for our succeeding generations.

Witness the fight to save the Ribble Estuary, to recover the Osprey in Scotland, and so on. Even early in your interest, you can contribute to the facts on which all conservation arguments must be based by expanding the study of your own place to meet the disciplines of the Common Bird Census. This scheme is also administered by the British Trust for Ornithology and provides an annual index of the bird populations of farmland and woodland. It involves the accurate mapping (on a 6″ scale) of all singing males within a set area of habitat during the breeding season; full details are available from the trust office, the address of which is given in the appendix.

Fieldcraft example: observer standing in "dead ground" and using broken rise to mask his presence, whilst counting geese in field ahead.

Next, your basic birdwatching kit. There are some unavoidable necessities, and the foremost is a good pair of binoculars. Without them, as any birdwatcher who has forgotten his knows, birds stay predominantly small or distant, or both. So you do face a sizeable investment (over £50) in adding extra optical power to your own visual acuity. Choosing binoculars is a matter for *much* trial and argument. Don't rush out and buy what the nearest shop recommends. Don't buy cheap or you will have to buy again. To begin with, try and borrow. Most families have a little used pair somewhere and with them (and the advice of other birdwatchers), you can assess your particular needs. Then it is a question of shopping around, obtaining models on a trial and approval basis, and buying *only* when you are fully satisfied with their optical performance (particularly the lack of distortion and brightness of image), their weight round your neck and balance in your hands, their comfort against your eyebrows or spectacles, and their robustness against the odd knock and constant weather. The birdwatcher tests binoculars to destruction; so steer clear of such complications as zoom lenses, which have a nasty habit of becoming loosely and unevenly geared. For most types of birdwatching, I recommend lens configurations of 9×35 or 10×40.

After a good pair of binoculars, the next thing you need is an accurate text on bird identification. I stress text before illustration for good reason; identification is rarely a matter of directly matching bird to plate. There is an almost embarrassingly wide choice of modern field guides. None is perfect but on balance I would choose the second oldest. This is *A Field Guide to the Birds of Britain and Europe*, first published 25 years ago and now in its third edition. Written by two British ornithologists, Guy Mountfort and Phillip Hollom, and illustrated by a leading American artist, Roger Peterson, it has stood the tests of accuracy better than its more recent and vivid competitors. I know this not only because I was involved in the revisions to both the second and third editions of "Peterson" (as it is usually called), but also because I have tried all the others and ended up by giving at least two away. Certainly "Peterson" will suffice for the needs of your first few years, during which you can judge the value of the other guides or more weighty tomes. The last are increasingly expensive but if your interest does run quickly towards the proving of new identification characters, they will be a worthwhile investment. Some are listed in the appendix to this book.

You must have a field notebook and a loose-leaf log. The former should be pocket size, sturdy and equipped with a rubber band to hold its pages still in the wind. The latter should be of sufficient size to accommodate a digest of your field notes, counts laid out in systematic order or scheduled against prepared lists of species (vertical) and dates (horizontal), and narrative entries about habitats or events. It is well worth spending more on your log than say the price of a large full page diary. For the last 19 years I have used Twinlock binders and both narrow- and box-ruled paper. They have stood multiple handling, reference, and even reconstruction better than any other. Be careful to transcribe quickly all the facts or impressions in your notebook to your log, or keep safe all your old field notes. One of my birdwatching tragedies has been the loss of all the records from my first nine years in the field.

You are now equipped to watch and study birds but you remain apart from other birdwatchers. So your next decision concerns membership of a local or national society, which will bring you into contact with more expert observers and give you the chance to go on conducted field meetings, to attend lectures, and to receive periodic literature including the annual bird report for your area or county. I suggest you start with your local society – most public libraries can tell you how to join – and get as much help as you can from members already experienced in the birds and habitats of your area. Remember, following too many other birdwatchers tends to lose you birds. The best fun (and science) comes in small group activity with shared objectives and effort.

During your initial learning period, you can also take up

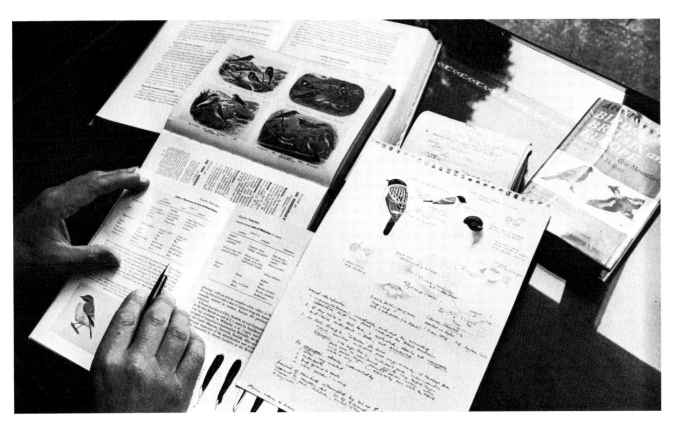

Homework example: "checking out" cock Siberian Stonechat seen at Flamborough Head on 1 May 1978. Field notes and drawings being checked against manuals and latest "BB" paper.

37

the opportunities of more formal training offered by the national organizations. The most help is offered by the British Trust for Ornithology. I have already mentioned their role in ringing and census work; they also issue a newsletter and a journal entitled *Bird Study,* organize the most informative (and popular) conferences for serious birdwatchers, and offer direct field training within the network of coastal bird observatories. Not everyone appreciates every word in the journal, but the support that the Trust commands among birdwatchers is immense. Over 10,000 observers contributed to its major corporate achievement, *The Atlas of Breeding Birds in Britain and Ireland.* Don't hesitate to join the B.T.O. the moment your interest and enthusiasm combines into a compulsive study. It could well provide the outlet for your results!

Other national societies offer the inexperienced birdwatcher much less substantial teaching than the B.T.O., but it is well worth supporting one of the essentially charitable organizations so important to the cause of conservation and the task of education in natural history. If you prefer to see your money go to several bodies, you may choose initially to switch your annual subscriptions between the Royal Society for the Protection of Birds and the Wildfowl Trust. Membership of these bodies directly assists the survival of birds and brings in tow the chance to visit some of the most marvellous bird reserves in the world. Slimbridge with its wild geese and swans and Minsmere with its Avocets and Marsh Harriers are not to be missed or lost through lack of finance in our inflationary society.

After these contacts you are left with only one other necessity, and it is not immediate. It is however very important. No birdwatcher can enjoy birds fully or develop into a field ornithologist without founding a library of books and journals, particularly those relevant to his or her preferred subjects. The choice in journals is easy. Not to receive the monthly riches of *British Birds* is sheer folly. Edited by five of Britain's leading ornithologists (all still active in the field) and published by Macmillan, "B.B." is the most readable and informative reference to current British Ornithology and attracts a wide readership. Most importantly it publishes notes and papers from amateur birdwatchers (who, like you, were once beginners) and so offers the best chance of an audience to your own research, always provided that it meets the tests of editorial criticism. "B.B." also has a special role in British ornithology. It administers or publishes the national disciplines on records of rare breeding birds and migrants. The reports on these are perhaps the most eagerly awaited of all annual announcements, for to many birdwatchers they contain the most important scores of each succeeding year.

Then there are the scientific handbooks, specific monographs, and other specialized literature. The choice is wide but unfortunately scarcity value or high publishing costs has vastly inflated their price in recent years. So initially, don't purchase any book other than that on your county's ornithology, which will provide the essential background to your own local studies. For others it is far more sensible to exert a heavy demand on your local library (which can often find even the most uncommon books) or the postal lending service of the B.T.O. If you cannot wait for outright ownership, then I would recommend the new authoritative and fact-jammed *Handbook of the Birds of Europe, the Middle East and North Africa,* being written by an international panel of editors and published by the Oxford University Press. The first volume appeared in 1978 and it will be a good decade before the seventh and last ends up on your bookshelf. But as a compendium of up-to-date knowledge and as an accurate portrayer of every species known to have occurred in the Western Palaearctic, the series is likely to have no equal for at least a century. Exaggeration perhaps, but being one of the editors, I am slightly biased.

You are now fully equipped to study birds and to add your observations to the general record. Whether you will add significantly to science is not certain. There is no reason why you shouldn't.

Great Places for Birds

By now I hope that you are eager to watch birds and determined to make a study of your own local community. However I cannot pretend that this will always be sufficient satisfaction for you. As your learning of the whole British avifauna grows, you will want to use it in a wider exploration of varying habitats and the birds that such supports. So in this chapter, I take you directly to seven of the great places for birds that I have visited. All have captured a piece of my ornithological heart; all will demonstrate for you some of the riches in your hobby.

In making the seven journeys for the book, I was joined by Philip Sayer and the photographic record is his work. Our travels began on Islay in March 1978 and ended in Regent's Park, London, in February 1979. All along the way, Phil questioned me on the essential content of the photographs and his full understanding of my often hasty answers shows marvellously in both the colour and black and white plates. They truly evoke both the places and the habitats within them.

I could not expect Phil to capture on film every bird that we saw. We had neither hide nor sufficient time for careful stalking and so settled for what birds came close. Where Phil was successful needs no pointing from me but I have added to his photographs coloured sketches of the main species that you should seek to discover. Please note that the subjects within these are not precisely scaled and thus are no substitute for the illustrations in your field guide. Now begin your journey.

Regent's Park in London

For a close look at common species and breeding Grey Herons.

Later in this chapter, we shall be going to some of the great wild places for birds which happily exist in Britain still. However for most birdwatchers, these can only be visited at weekends or on longer holidays. So if you want to enter the world of birds regularly (and I have argued that you should), it is best to find a varied habitat close to your home and visit it frequently. Such places exist within most of our conurbations; they are the often gracious gardens and parks that the early decorators of our cities wisely saw fit to create or preserve. Thus, even the most urban birdwatcher can keep contact with more than just sparrows, Starlings and pigeons, and the occasional observation of some uncommon species will be all the more exciting against the backdrop of the encliffed stone gullies that is Man's main habitat in the bird's eye.

To demonstrate this point, Phil and I went on a raw February day to my favourite green space in any city,

Inner London and Regent's Park, from Primrose Hill. During autumn gales, migrants pass low over summit.

Regent's Park in London. Its 600 acres contain a wide variety of habitats, and a walk to the top of abutting Primrose Hill gets you up into the sky and affords a breathtaking panorama of ancient monuments dodging new office blocks and tourist hotels, the lie of the Thames Valley and the North Downs. To the ordinary passer-by, the park offers grass to be green, flowers to strike colours, a lake to bear splashing boats, and so on; but to birds (and you), it is a small discrete oasis in an urban badland. Since birds have no consciousness of its artificiality, they simply exploit its suitability as much as possible. Thus the individual habitats in Regent's Park attract at least some part of the profile of species that occur in them in more natural situations. Furthermore the essentially broadfront character of bird movements ensures that such are often visible, too.

During the morning hours of our visit, Phil and I were surprised by a continuous passage of Skylarks towards the north-east (probably stimulated by the temporary thaw of the period), the tameness of Magpies which allowed us within 10 yards (try matching that anywhere near a gamekeeper), and by the competitiveness of a Great Spotted Woodpecker trying to sound out his territorial drum loud enough to pierce the traffic's rumble. We were also held almost spellbound by the antics of the world's most urban Grey Herons, busy attending to their huge stick nests and indulging in bouts of courting. The events that we witnessed were typical of the many close contacts with birds that I have found especially heightened by the urban circumstance of the observation.

The study that I made of the birds of Regent's Park from 1958 to 1965 is likely to remain the core of my whole ornithological experience. For almost two out of three days for the seven years, my day began with a walk there before breakfast and work, and I made many other visits on a fuller stomach. The sum of my observations and those of various helpers was remarkable; over 100 species discovered in all, nearly 40 breeding and over 40 wintering. Many farming habitats could not compete with those scores, or provide the variety of birds that they imply. So you need not fear boredom if most of your birdwatching has to be done in city or town. Nothing has lasted me better than the pleasures of having seen, in the middle of London's sprawl, Smews from Northern Scandinavia and a Bewick's Swan from Siberia, of having witnessed the return as breeding species of Grey Heron, Coal Tit, Blackcap and Magpie, and of knowing (just about) where every resident bird was and what it was doing. I should have seen one amazing rarity, but alas the April morning that a Blackeared Wheatear reached the park (instead of Spain) and entranced two friends, I took a lie in!

Adult drake Tufted Duck in breeding plumage; some wintering in Regent's Park depart as far as N. Russia to breed. Bill pattern unique to species.

Particularly if the wind blows up from the north-west in late autumn, the dawn sky over Primrose Hill can be packed with flocks of migrants journeying from the Low Countries to the moist centre and west of Southern England. The most dramatic movements are of the ubiquitous Starling and that rather underrated bird, the Wood Pigeon. The migrations of the latter remain ill-defined, but in early November of some years thousands per hour fly purposefully west over London.

To a beginner in ornithology, there are many benefits in studying a place like Regent's Park. The initial diversity of species is unlikely to be bewildering, the birds themselves tend to be used to human disturbance and therefore tamer, and the problems of grasping the fundamental character of the habitats and their avian inhabitants will be of a span that should not defeat keen eyes and a reasoning mind. Thus you will soon see that the wild Tufted Ducks of each winter may quickly learn to take bread from your fingers but still retire to a safe roost out on the lake at night; that the insectivorous and granivorous birds like tits and Chaffinches will prefer shrubberies, tree canopies and the winter wreck of flower beds; and that the football pitches that may appear as bald as Derby County's infamous Baseball Ground may yet contain sufficient invertebrates to attract a Wheatear in spring or Linnets in winter. Learning such lessons is all important

43

Regent's Park's Herons probably came from the heronries at Walthamstow

Grey Heron

largest dark bird in English sky

"fish spear"

adult

Sexes similar

NB white crescents on upperwing

Wings "clap" on take off

Wood Pigeon

long legs for wading

always looks chesty

"London" Pigeon

descended from wild Rock Dove

Black-headed Gull

adult in summer

adult in winter

NB dusky underwing, with white leading edge

ubiquitous, common in winter

Starling

always busy

usually chattering

plumage iridescent

cock

Dunnock

alias **Hedge Sparrow**

but actually an accentor

Lesser Blackbacked Gull

NB yellow legs

as Herring Gull, occasionally breeds in London parks

calls "peek" piercingly

feeds under hedges

Carrion Crow
Long known in town parks

Crows

sexes similar in all crows

Magpie

Chatters

now entering towns

Kestrel   male

hovers, then drops onto small rodents

Blackcap   cock

hen has "browncap"

Song rich and fluting, more pronounced than that of Garden Warbler

Black-eared Wheatear

cock

only 16 have reached Britain, 1 Regent's Park!

Wheatear
cock in spring

white rump, common to most wheatears

Meadow Pipit

calls "tseep" in alarm

common migrant over London, drops down to green spaces

cock

feeds along edges of waters

Pied Wagtail

commonest in Britain

calls "chiz-zick"

Wren

seeks food everywhere at ground level, like mouse

suffers badly in cold winters

song vibrant, clear and very loud for size of utterer

*Regent's Park: "gardened" habitat always
affording shelter and food. Liked by Bullfinches;
last refuge of London's Wrens in cruel 1962/1963
winter.*

to a wide understanding of birds and their ways of life,
without which any leaning that you feel towards the more
scientific aspects of birdwatching can hardly be confirmed.
There really is no better school of birdwatching than that
exhibited in your nearest park. Why not enrol tomorrow?

Getting there

Regent's Park has its own tube station at its south-east
corner. Other areas of the park are much more quickly
approached from Baker Street, St. John's Wood and Camden
Town. Car-parking is tricky with the free-for-all of past years
now a maze of timed zones, but the north-west quadrant of
the Inner Circle is usually open. There, you are just minutes
from the herons on the island at the mouth of the north-east
reach of the lake.

Once you are finished with the birds of the park and Primrose Hill, you should consider whether the value of any long
journey that misses out a visit to the zoo is sufficient. Remember my early advice and try at least to see the bird
collection which is mostly situated along the eastern edge.
Sadly, some of the individuals in the aviaries show the wear
and tear of captivity, but that is no reason to ignore the
ready display and close proximity of more early lessons in
appearance, relationships, and occasionally behaviour.

Islay

For wild geese, uncommon crows, and Black Grouse.

Generally the further out the place, the fewer its people and the least disturbed its animals. In Britain this rule broadly applies on a south-east to north-west axis and I cannot but include one of the Hebridean islands in my short list of great places for birds. I got to know several in the summers of my youth and even managed to stumble over St. Kilda before its one road. However, the journeys to such isolation approach expedition proportions and in choosing Islay for an appearance in this book, I was swayed not just by its marvellous birds but also by its relative proximity.

Circle Islay, the most southerly of all the Hebrides, from the sea and you will see the grey shores, black cliffs, and buff and brown hills typical of all of western Scotland. Go ashore and you will also find yellow mosses, pale green fields, dark green gorse and woods, and black peat cuttings. More than any other Hebridean island, its confusing configuration means that each turn of the road brings a new vista. When the sky is blue and high, the colours of Islay dance and even when the sky is grey and low, they are not completely subdued. The purple tones of the winter birch appear the most intense in the world. For these reasons, and her mild winter

Sunset over Loch Indaal, Islay; watching roosting flights of geese, gulls and waders.

Loch Gorm; freshwater supporting swans and allowing seagulls to wash their plumages. Hen Harriers over moss; Choughs near cliffs.

climate, Islay is crowned Queen of the Hebrides. She lacks high hills but even these are provided by the Paps of neighbouring Jura, which dominate the northern horizon. Once joined to both Ireland and Argyll, Islay is an old place. Yet within a few miles, you can walk from some of the oldest rocks in Britain to estate woodland hand-made in the nineteenth century. Even the intense farming of the fertile limestone heart of the island has added to the beautiful variety of Islay. Recently Man has retreated from living in the marginal farms and cottages, but in fine weather it remains a soft, simple place which refreshes every visitor.

To you in your discovery of birds, Islay is first and foremost the greatest goose ground in Britain. About 25,000 winter in its 235 square miles. Nowhere else will you see so many so easily, nowhere else will you get so close to them so often, and nowhere else will their winter ecology be so simple to understand. From October to early April, all large areas of grass on Islay, and particularly those between the heads of the two sea lochs which almost divide the island, have flocks of geese on them or flying between them. The commonest is the Barnacle Goose, a rather small grass-nibbling species with a striking black, grey, and white plumage pattern. Islay is the winter home of the biggest community of the Barnacle Goose in the world, that which breeds in Greenland. In recent years the counts of the community conducted by the Wildfowl Trust have added up to more than 20,000. Except on the high tops and along the eastern coastline, Barnacle Geese are about you all the time. If you want to enjoy them to the full, don't miss their arrival at dusk at their main roost at Bridgend. There the quiet salt marshes and mudflats attract an evening flight of thousands and seen against the setting sun, it is as vital and memorable as any scene from the game plains of Serengeti. The barking chorus of the birds adds a dimension in sound that only the goose watcher enjoys.

The next commonest goose in Islay is the Whitefronted Goose, a rather large grass- and root-eating species with a dark brown variegated plumage pattern, set off by a white forehead and marvellously orange bill, legs and feet. The Whitefront is even more ubiquitous on Islay than the Barnacle but because it tends to feed in the flooded hollows of fields, among rushes and other tall ground vegetation, and occurs in smaller flocks, it is not as obvious. Six other geese occur on Islay but only one other, the Grey Lag, is regular. Up to 200, probably coming south from the Outer Hebrides, are found. Of the rest, two are particularly attractive to the birdwatcher. These are the occasional truly wild Snow Goose and Canada Goose that appear amongst the Barnacles and Whitefronts. These are lost singletons that have strayed east from their breeding grounds in Canada in early autumn, joined their cousins on their southward migration from Greenland, and so reached Islay in their company. Usually such exceptional rarities appear only once, but in recent years a splendid blue phase Snow Goose has become a permanent member of a small flock of Whitefronts that haunt the rushy grass at Avenvogie. On the ground its white head shines like a beacon.

Wild geese make such splendid sights and noises that they are hard to forsake, but there are many other birds on Islay. At least 224 different species have been recorded, and of these, at least 110 have bred. If you go to Islay in the summer, I recommend that you concentrate on the crows. All seven British species have reached the island and five are breeding residents. Two are of the essence of coastal and upland wilderness, the Raven and the Chough. The second, you must not miss.

Although now rare in Britain, the Chough is tame, inquisitive and even perhaps disdainful of Man. More than any other crow, it is a bird of supreme confidence in the air and its structure for flight (long broad wings with well spaced

Some of Islay's 20,000 Barnacle Geese, but how many? Make your estimate, then check it by individual count.

49

Chough

bill fine, red
like feet

Jet black far off,
iridescent close to

party
tumbling
down cliffs

Golden
Eagle

immature

White in
wings and tail
absent in
adult

huge,
majestic

wings held in
shallow V

hen
dark brown

Shows
"ringtail"

adult

Barnacle Geese
wary flock on skyline

immature

adults,
with 'whitefronts'

Greeland
Whitefronted

large
bill for
pulling up
roots as
well as grass,
orange
like feet

Blue Snow

adult

Small dark falcon,
catches small birds
in rapid chase

Merlin

hen

Hen Harrier

cock
grey

belly
barred black

adult

immature,
with
speckled
face

Greyhen

Blackcocks

Barnacle

Small bill
for nibbling
short grass,
black like
legs and feet

Pinkfooted

bill pink
like feet

Barnacle

head of
adult

Black Grouse

tail spread
in display

Wild geese present
October to April

Scaup

dense flock often off Bowmore

ducks brown, with white faces

drake

duck

large, heavy

listen for cooing chorus, from drakes in spring

Eider

Peregrine

NB white shoulders of drake

large powerful falcon, black cap and moustache.

Wigeon in flight

stoops on other birds

drake

both sexes show ragged crest

NB long "sawbill" for fish catching

white neck more obvious than red breast

young drake

adult drake

Small bill for grazing

drake

duck

Pintail

large bill for dabbling

Swims low in water

duck

Red-breasted Merganser

Red-throated Diver

thin upturned bill, held up

adult in winter

duck

long thin tail, hence name

large "dagger" held level

Wigeon

often in dense packs on grass

scarce, but often at Ardnave

Great Northern Diver

immature

pointed tail and wing-tips obvious as bird dives

Black Guillemot, alias Tystie

brown-black in summer, except for white wing-coverts

fish-eating divers and grebes usually on sea, often in Loch Indaal

NB gleaming white cheeks contrasting with dark crown

"tailless"

winter plumage

mostly white in winter

on sea, near low cliffs

Slavonian Grebe

"fingers" and full tail) reflects its ability to float and wheel and tumble in all the airs from Western Ireland to the furthest mountains of Asia. The Chough is the sort of bird that makes the world seem smaller than even that flown by Concorde. On Islay, it often joins together with the Jackdaw which, though a considerable character, is dull by comparison. When you are in company with the Chough, look especially for the narrow decurved red bill with which the bird probes expertly in grass, around rocks and patches of earth, or in animal droppings; and perceive how that product of specific evolution allows it a specialist niche in the search for food. Its legs and feet are also red, and in almost any light the plumage of the Chough is beautifully sheeny. What at any distance is a jet black bird proves, close to the eye, to be clothed in blue, green and purple gloss. Listen, too, for the merry shouted *kiaow* that the Chough gives, a bird call to turn your head and make your heart pound. The Chough may be seen almost anywhere in Islay, but don't search the cliffs on which they nest. Be content with waiting for them to come to you in Machire Bay, where they feed on the grassy dunes, or along the cliffs and uplands of the seaboard of the Rhinns.

One other bird deserves special mention, and that is the Black Grouse. This fine gamebird, the male called the Blackcock and the female the Greyhen, is widespread on Islay, favouring the tussock and grass edges of plantations and patches of scrub in heather. In my experience, it shows itself more readily on Islay than anywhere else in Scotland, giving you the chance to enjoy another truly beautiful bird. The Blackcock has glossy blue-black plumage set off by white in the wing and under its lyre-shaped tail, so often worn as a bonnet plume by Scottish soldiers. The Greyhen is all brown and grey, a miracle of camouflage. Look especially for groups of Blackcocks at dawn and dusk and you may see the display known as the lek. This is a form of sexual competition that insures that only the finest and fittest males carry the line on.

South of Barr; conifer plantation sheltering Black Grouse, streambed birches harbouring passerines, and fields attracting "grey" geese.

Phil and I were on Islay on two March days; the first as crystal clear as only a western day can be; the second grey or normal but still calm. We did very well, and several of the other birds that we saw or that are usually visible on Islay are indicated in the accompanying sketches. Given only a few days of less than "solid lash" (heavy rain in the ornithological vernacular), you should see them all. All you will need is the 1″ Ordnance Survey map and the excellent *Birds in Islay*, by Gordon Booth. Together these provide an exhaustive guide to the island and its bird habitats. Even if rain and wind does keep you in your car, you may well see 100 different species in a day, and that is an achievement anywhere in Britain.

Barnacle Goose and Greenland Whitefronted Goose, south of Ardnave. Former usually in large flocks on short grass, latter in small parties often in rushy field bottoms.

Getting there

Starting from Glasgow, there is a two-hour drive to Tarbert via the A82 beside Loch Lomond and the A83 down the west shore of Loch Fyne. From the West Loch at Tarbert roll on-roll off ferries, operated by the Caledonian Mac-Brayne and Western lines, sail respectively for Port Ellen and Port Askaig. To enjoy a full weekend, you should stay overnight at a hotel in Tarbert and catch the 0630 sailing on Saturday, arriving at Islay within $2\frac{1}{2}$ hours. A return sailing at 1600 on Sunday is convenient for an evening withdrawal to Glasgow. (Check that timetables haven't changed.) By the way, get your binoculars out immediately you board the ferry. In winter, the West Loch has all three British divers in it for a start.

55

The Isles of Scilly

For almost any bird on the British list.

Land's End is not the most south-westerly point of England. Bishop Rock with its proud lighthouse is. Scattered to the east of this last stone shelf is the beautiful archipelago called the Isles of Scilly. Brought up on (and indoctrinated with) Scottish hills and isles, I hardly knew of their existence before 1955 but following their exploration by some Cambridge and London friends, I was finally dragooned into service at the bird observatory on the smallest island, St. Agnes, in 1959. In the last two decades, I have gone back to the archipelago almost every year. The reason is quite clear. Nowhere else have I found such exhilaration from prettiness of place, pleasure in people, and bounty of birds. To wander among the islands (by motor launch, bicycle and foot, never car) is often to have the complete birdwatching experience. Why and how? Because nowhere in the whole world do the birds of the Holarctic region so constantly intermingle as in Scilly (never *Scillies!*), and this annual autumn happening has made the archipelago one of the most famous places of ornithological pilgrimage. True Fair Isle, between Orkney and Shetland, still holds the record for the most extraordinary rarities from Eurasia, but Scilly has so far produced about

Bishop Rock lighthouse from St. Agnes. Flown round by common and rare seabirds; Oyster Catchers disturbed from high-tide roost.

325 out of a total of 485 birds on the British list. There is no real duel for birdwatching honour between the two poles of rarity finding in Britain, but there is an enjoyable vein of competition in the discussion of what each annually scores!

The reasons why Scilly produces so many rare and uncommon birds are not difficult to isolate. Firstly, just as Britain and Ireland form the last bulwarks to Europe and so screen many birds moving over or wandering away from the continental landmass, so do the Isles of Scilly serve as a whole fleet of lifeboats for migrants over the surrounding seas. On clear days in spring and autumn, the islands are usually over-flown – the 25 miles between Land's End and St. Mary's represents little more than a bustling half hour for a Starling – but in mixed or bad weather, at any time of the year, they are used as a ready haven by hundreds, even thousands of birds.

Boulder cairns, St. Agnes, Scilly; observer studying family of Stonechats in nearby gorse patch; dog "Sheba" keener on ratting but to heel.

57

Secondly, once birds have fallen into Scilly, they are often very obvious. The main agricultural produce of the human community combines early flowers with early vegetables, and the small high-hedged fields needed to protect those sensitive crops from winter storms also offer ideal resting and feeding areas to tired, hungry birds all the year round. Indeed much of Scilly forms the bird garden *par excellence*. Thirdly, the total finding effort put in by 200 or 300 birdwatchers throughout the autumns of recent years is probably the most intensive in Britain. Regular observers have learnt even the very best trees and coves for birds, let alone the most productive island or sound, and the bird harvest of Scilly is now skilfully taken in. Fourthly, the geographical position of

the archipelago means that just as the anchorage seeking galleons of the Armada became wrecked there, so many birds that have found the Atlantic stretching too far beneath them also make desperate landfalls. Some of these waifs come incredible distances, and the most surprising are the small multitudes of Nearctic waders and passerines that so often appear out of Atlantic storms. Nowhere else in Britain and Ireland have so many been seen. All in all, islands behave as huge binoculars and so serve the migration watcher as more acute lenses than any other habitat. Those of Scilly allow an astonishingly close focus.

It is impossible for me to list all that you might see, but some of the star attractions must be given credit. One of the most frequent American waders to appear in Scilly is the delicate Buff-breasted Sandpiper. To reach its favourite haunt, the short grass of St. Mary's Airport, this bird must fly over half of Canada and the whole Atlantic. Yet, amazingly, it is as regular there as anywhere on the coast of New England. In a good year (of high breeding success and strong westerly winds), even flocks appear. With the Buffbreasts may come Pectoral Sandpipers and other closely related migrant waders. However these are such superb fliers that their appearances stun less than those of American landbirds. Many of these have gaudier plumages than Eurasian passerines, and to see a bright sprite like a Myrtle Warbler or the

North-west beaches and Big Pool, St. Agnes. Look particularly on Periglis (right) for Nearctic waders, wait by pool for glimpses of migrant rails.

Yearling Turnstones in almost full breeding plumage, showing unique flight pattern that makes their identification simple, unlike most birds!

Great Blackbacked Gull

preys on smaller seabirds

adult

winters in open sea

immature

immature

adults

Kittiwake

calls its name, nests on cliff ledges

Roseate Tern

very long tail streamers "whip" in flight

adult in summer

always looks whiter than Common

Buffbreasted Sandpiper

Common Tern

in autumn both cross Atlantic

git tripping and elegant

underparts pink in adult when breeding

Pectoral Sandpiper

immature in autumn

NB wide chest band of streaks

present May to October

Sanderling

hovers, then plunges for small fish

palest of small waders: always running, so has lost hind-toe

immature in autumn

adults in breeding dress

wings flutter

calls "tit"

immatures in autumn

adults in winter

chuckles staccato

NB white Vs on chestnut back

calls "quib"

Turnstone

really tiny!

Little Stint

does just that to find food

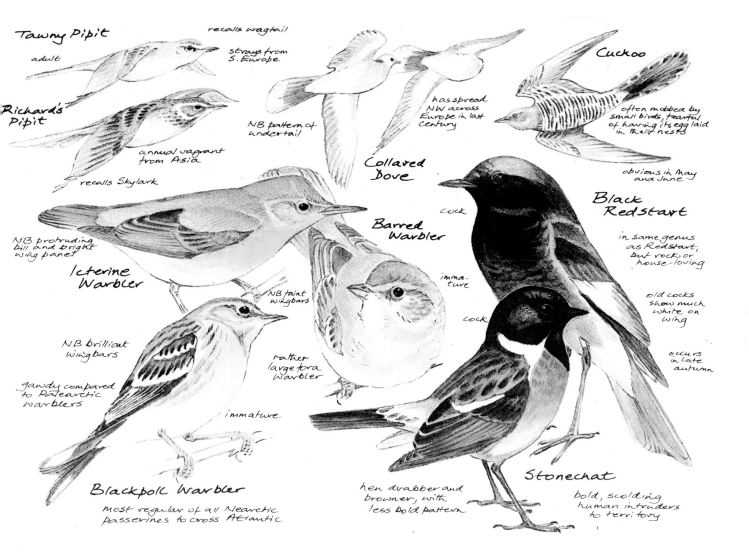

Tawny Pipit

adult

recalls wagtail

strays from S. Europe

Richard's Pipit

annual vagrant from Asia

recalls Skylark

NB pattern of undertail

Collared Dove

has spread NW across Europe in last century

Cuckoo

often mobbed by small birds, fearful of having its egg laid in their nests

obvious in May and June

Black Redstart

in same genus as Redstart, but rock- or house-loving

old cocks show much white on wing

occurs in Late autumn

NB protruding bill and bright wing panel

Icterine Warbler

NB faint wingbars

NB brilliant wingbars

Barred Warbler

cock

imma-ture

rather large for a warbler

gaudy compared to Palearctic warblers

immature

cock

Blackpoll Warbler

Most regular of all Nearctic passerines to cross Atlantic

hen drabber and browner, with less bold pattern

Stonechat

bold, scolding human intruders to territory

incredibly striped Black and White Warbler snapping up flies 3,500 miles away from their intended point of arrival in the Caribbean or South America is a miraculous experience. The latter bird is the nearest thing to a feathered zebra, but it is tiny by comparison, weighing about 15 grammes. And it flies the Atlantic!

Not every Scilly day contains an American bird but there are almost always others from elsewhere in the compass quarters. From the north, you may see the odd vagrant that has overshot its normal winter range. Once on St. Agnes, a breathlessly ecstatic observer burst into the observatory, gulped and stuttered, "There's a Snow-Snow-Snow-"; we all expected him to finish with "Bunting" but what he finally got out was "-y Owl!" The mass exodus from tea (the birdwatcher's elixir) was instant and complete. I broke the world landspeed record for fathers pushing babies in prams, and there in the bracken of Gugh was the most magnificent beast that any of us had ever seen: an adult Snowy Owl, and no mistake. From the south-west, you may see not only seabirds like Cory's Shearwater from mid-Atlantic islands but also Spanish passerines like Melodious Warbler, Tawny Pipit and Blackeared Wheatear. From the south may come a Mediterranean falcon such as Lesser Kestrel, a huge Alpine Swift, or a tiny golden Serin. From any direction to the east, the chances of a truly unusual bird are even wider. Among

Cropped flower pieces of St. Agnes; part of Britain's greatest "bird garden". The disused lighthouse has twice been circled by Alpine Swifts from Spain.

the commoner migrants like familiar Chiffchaffs and Chaffinches may be buff-grey Barred Warblers from Germany, a pale-naped Rustic Bunting from Finland, a gem-like Pallas's Leaf Warbler from central Asia, a hulking Richard's Pipit from the same area, or an immature Rose-coloured Starling from the Levant. All in all, the next bird in Scilly may be rare and the one after that usually is!

On the days when the birdwatching fever on the islands subsides (because rarities are absent), you are free to enjoy the resident bird population or watch the less fickle European waders and gulls. In the former, look particularly at the local Dunnocks. Do they look to you browner than those in your garden or park? They do to me, and they may well be a distinct island race. Yet to my knowledge, no ornithologist has yet proved this or even investigated it. Amongst the latter, don't miss the constantly sprinting back and forth Sanderlings which feed on the invertebrates exposed by the surf of each wave, or the bustling, chuckling Turnstones that swarm on rocks or seaweed wracks. Neither of these delightful Arctic waders breed in Scilly but there are only a few days of the year when some are not present there.

If you go to Scilly in summer, don't forget to enjoy two of the most graceful birds in the world, the Common and Roseate Terns. The former breeds on several isles and rocks, the latter on only two. The best place to see them together is the south shore of Tresco. You will find the nesting area in the dunes enclosed but a patient watch from nearby cover should bring the desired results of contact *and* nil disturbance. Just avoid the spring mist that beat off Phil's attempt at photography in our May visit.

Getting there

The best point of departure for Scilly is Penzance. There you have the choice of the R.M.S. *Scillonian,* flat-bottomed, shallow-draught and awkward in heavy seas, but often close to all sorts of seabirds; or the British Airways helicopter, noisy, faster (20 minutes, not $2\frac{3}{4}$ hours), nervous of fog, and too far above seabirds on most passes. Both take you to the main island of St. Mary's, whence launches leave from Hugh Town to the outer isles. Accommodation is tight. So book well in advance.

The best map is the $2\frac{1}{2}''$ Ordnance Survey and the most useful written guide to the birds is the annual *Scilly Bird Report,* edited by Harry Robinson and David Hunt. The latter is resident on St. Mary's and must answer more birdwatcher's questions than anyone else in Britain.

Flamborough

For seabirds on the cliffs and over the sea.

No other piece of land sticks out from the east coast of England like Flamborough Head. For me, it marks the divide of the soft south from the hard north of the country, and for years I mused on the birds that might be there. I never thought to know. Since 1972, however, I have lived within 40 miles of the head and I now escape there more than anywhere else. It is a magnificent place. Both its sides are huge white walls of degraded limestone and together they thrust the promontory across the coastal currents and out into the North Sea. The cliffs are skirted with a seaweed-strewn rock shelf, and the table of the headland is carpeted with fields, hedges and woods. An ancient earthwork called Danes Dyke cuts north to south across it, and east of this wooded defile there is an island feel to the place. The very end is graced by one very old and one not so old lighthouse, and shattered occasionally by an appallingly loud foghorn. Sitting there you are effectively six miles out to sea.

The last fact is responsible for the main ornithological news story to be told of Flamborough Head. Particularly since 1976, a growing effort in the observation of passing seabirds, known as "seawatching", shows every sign of forcing

North cliffs. Home of thousands of seabirds constantly commuting between their nests and the small fish in the sea.

the revision of the status of most marine species known in the North Sea. A small group of observers, braving all weathers and almost always there at dawn, keep on producing surprises; the passages that they have seen, for example of Sooty Shearwaters from the South Atlantic, Longtailed Skuas from the summer tundra, and the supposedly very rare Little Shearwaters from the eastern mid-Atlantic, have provoked the usual sequence of scepticism, argument and acceptance in the national record. Particularly when the wind blows briskly from anywhere between NW and E, seabirds can pass Flamborough Head in such densities that sometimes we have to divide the duties of observation and count notation.

North Sea at dawn, from Flamborough Head: sea-watching in progress.

If you come to Flamborough Head, look for the sea-watchers sitting on the grass ledges below the foghorn. You are free to sit by them but try to interrupt their study as little as possible. The current leading observer, Andrew Lassey, is a very helpful interpreter of the scene, but because the study is still in the discovery stage his concentration is likely to switch quickly back to the sea whenever birds fly by.

Profitable seawatching is possible on many other head-lands, promontories, and even on straight coastlines. The major factor that makes seabirds visible from land is onshore wind, but poor visibility at sea and high waves clearly add to their displacement by obscuring the land. The most famous station for seawatching is Cape Clear in south-west Ireland, but I advocate no such travels before you have built up some experience. The rules are simple. Always watch the sea from a fixed station (or a close series of least windy nooks); find out where most birds first appear (this will vary with the direction of the wind, into which most birds move head-on) and start your scans of the sea from those points; look closely at every bird that appears and learn as soon as possible the structural and flight characters of the common seabirds like Kittiwakes and Fulmars; store them mentally so that any unusual sil-houette can be quickly spotted; and do not forget to write your counts and identification notes throughout the watch (not at the end).

Four species co-habiting on cliff: Kittiwake preening on nest (top left), *Rock Dove below nest hole* (top right), *Puffins and adult Guillemots with chicks* (bottom).

On the east coast, the rising sun can be a nuisance in the early morning; on the west coast, it is so at night. Looking into it, you will not see much of any plumage pattern. This can be frustrating, but as your skill mounts you may actually welcome the clarity of silhouette that back light allows. The identification of passing seabirds is no mean task. You are bound to make mistakes early on (and later), but getting as much advice as possible will keep the puzzle level down to a minimum. Do try seawatching, it is a great sport and a good way to relax from the more active tactics necessary for most landbird observations.

There is another story to be told of seabirds at Flamborough and it concerns the breeding gulls, auks, Shags and Gannets that occupy the ledges of its northern cliffs in summer, and together make up one of the largest seabird communities in Europe. The population of Kittiwakes alone is close to 100,000 pairs. To see them and secure some of them on film, Phil and I visited the R.S.P.B. reserve at Bempton twice in late summer, but on both occasions fog beat the camera. Finally we did find the sun at Breil Nook in late July and the results are self-evident in the accompanying photographs. Don't miss the seabird cauldron of Breil Nook when you come to Flamborough. It swirls with Shags, Kittiwakes, Guillemots, Razorbills, Puffins, Fulmars, Rock Doves and Jackdaws in every month from March to July. If

Part of Breil Nook, Flamborough Head; accommodating hundreds of Kittiwakes, Guillemots and other cliff-nesting species. All shun lower ledges exposed to egg-removing spray.

67

Sabine's Gull

Same wing pattern at all ages, but immature brown above where adult grey

tern-like flight

Gannet

all adults

wing-span 6'; crash-dives for fish

flutters wings almost continuously

Little Shearwater

NB dark eye on white face, unlike Manx's dark half-hood

wings and tail usually carried above water

Longtailed Skua

on Arctic tundra in summer

adults

adult lacks white wing marks of other skuas

NB long tail streamers

Arctic Skua

all skuas make other seabirds give up food, after fierce piratical chase

breeds in W. and N. Scotland

Sooty Shearwater

NB all dark primaries on Manx, unlike Little

Manx Shearwater

adult and immature similar

Great Skua alias Bonxie

Huge, powerful; often chases Gannets

breeds in N. Scotland

Great Shearwater

all alternate glides with flaps,

sometimes wheel and soar

underwing silvery

uncommon Shearwaters present April to October; then go south into Atlantic to breed

Fulmar

common on all northern and western coasts

feet sometimes assist tail in steering

Fieldfare
rather large

both "winter thrushes", arriving in September

Redwing
actually Redflank

rather small

sexes similar

song suggests rattle of keys

both resident

Corn Bunting
feet often trail in flight

commonest bunting

cock

Rustic Bunting

rare, May and autumn

sings: "Little bit of bread - and no cheese"

both cocks

Yellowhammer
both sexes

long-tailed, like most of buntings

NB bills of Shrikes hooked, for flesh eating

cock

Red-backed Shrike

Summer visitor, preys on insects and small reptiles

NB striking tail pattern

chases bumble-bees

Sexes similar

NB two toes forward, two back

Wryneck
closely related to woodpeckers, but migrants often perch on fences and feed on ground

black and white wings and tail obvious in flight

Great Grey Shrike

winter visitor, maintains hunting territory

cock

Ring Ouzel
breeds on hillsides

Summer visitor and passage migrant

hen browner

it is the lordly Gannet that you want to see, you must go to Bempton. About 150 pairs of this great white bird, with golden head and black wing-tips, breed on some broad ledges about half a mile west of the car park. Do also take your time to look not just at the great mass of birds in the cliff city but also at small groups and individuals. You will see Puffins flying in with shining sand eels held across their multi-coloured bills, young Kittiwakes exercising their untried wings or careering off on their initiation into flight, and Razorbills shuffling into the crevices that they (and not Guillemots) prefer. Such observations will make sense of the astonishing variety of specific behaviour within the mass reproduction of the community.

Much more can be said of Flamborough Head which is clearly set to rival Spurn as old Yorkshire's (or new Humberside's) most productive place for rare birds. However most of the land is private and general access for birdwatchers is restricted to a privileged few. If you come in autumn to watch the sea, do also try for migrants along the southern cliff path, at South Landing, and in the south end of Danes Dyke. However if such become your main target, I advise a visit to North Norfolk.

Juvenile Kittiwakes practising flight control alongside several storeys of natal colony.

Getting there

Flamborough Head is best approached via Bridlington, whence the B1255 leads you past Sewerby and Danes Dyke and on to the narrowing head. There are car parks at the south end of the dyke, South Landing, and by the younger lighthouse. The last is only a few minutes' walk from the seawatch station.

A final word of warning, the cliffs of Flamborough Head are the most dangerous that I have ever sat on. They erode continually and demand the greatest care in your steps. Every year several people fall to their death; so be very careful.

Adult Fulmars in mutual display and guttural duet (bottom left) and brooding chick (top centre).

Rothiemurchus and the Cairngorms

For birds of pine and birch forest, heather and the high tops, especially the Osprey.

Towards the ends of land, be they islands, coastal promontories or high mountains, the diversity of bird populations lessens and most numbers fall. Fewer habitat zones mean fewer niches for birds, and particularly where climate is made seasonally extreme by an increase in altitude, the successful species have, through natural selection, become adapted either to cope with the whole set of annual hazards or to exploit rapidly the increased food sources and brief calm of summer. In Britain it is debatable whether there is any alpine habitat in a strict sense, but heavy snow and wind chill make the summits of the higher Scottish mountains come close enough to sustain some (and currently attract a few more) Alpine or tundra species. Certainly it is well worth making an upwards trek in hill country to see the lowland birds drop away and be greeted by the distinctive upland ones that take over. The easiest place to do this in Britain is Speyside, where the western shoulders of the vast Cairngorm massif rise steeply from the ancient heaths and conifers of Rothiemurchus.

Phil and I went to the Cairngorms in late July and enjoyed

North-west shoulder, Cairngorm mountain;
vantage point over the Rothiemurchus forest.

Cathedral of Loch an Eilean; home of last
19th-century Ospreys and still surrounded by
Scotland's forest birds.

a long day there. It began at dawn at Loch an Eilean with a fierce silvery mist etching out even the thickest trunks of the surrounding woods, continued in the sun-filled and soon baking glades of the outer forest, but ended rather abruptly in a cold grey mist that inexorably pressed us down from the north-west shoulder of Cairngorm itself. The sudden coming of bad weather was disappointing but we could not take the risk of becoming disorientated, lost, and a nuisance to the local mountain rescue team. So we "abseiled" down the ski-lift, watching the marvellous panorama of the Spey Valley coming up to meet us again.

The woods of Rothiemurchus are both young and planted and old and self-regenerating. The latter have held safe during the past centuries of deforestation in Scotland a profile of conifer-loving birds (unique in Britain). They are only erratic in their appearances elsewhere; so you must take your chance of them fully here. Explore the wild woods slowly for they have a lot to offer. Great Scot Firs are everywhere, some gaunt and skeletal, others in their prime, and young ones just sprays of pine needles. The older trees in particular harbour the rarest breeding tit in Britain, the rather sombre coloured but fabulously behatted Crested Tit. This relative of the commoner tits requires decaying conifer stumps in which to excavate its nest hole and so finds Rothiemurchus ideal. Nowadays the Crested Tit shows signs of

spreading into reafforestated areas but your best chance of finding it quickly is in Rothiemurchus. Look out too for the Coal Tit, a veritable sprite with a bold white spot on its black nape and a piercing call.

While searching for the tits, you may notice small flocks of heavy-headed, rather sparrow-like finches overhead, calling *chup-chup-chup* and showing forked ends to their tails as they pass by. These belong to another group of passerines even more strictly associated with conifers and possessing an extraordinary bill with crossed mandibles (upper and lower halves), evolved to extract seeds from cones. Once again they are aptly named, Crossbills. Until recently ornithologists

Edge of Rothiemurchus forest. Look for owls at dawn and dusk, Greenshanks in pools and both common pipits.

used to argue about whether they were a form of the Common Crossbill, widely dispersed among the conifers of Europe, or a race of the more northerly Parrot Crossbill. The current balance of opinion, recognizing the long isolation of the resident birds in Scotland, is that they are a species in their own right. If this is confirmed by fuller research, the Scottish Crossbill and *not* the Red Grouse (in fact only a race of the Willow Grouse of Northern Europe) will be Britain's only truly indigenous bird. Crossbills get frequent thirsts from their dry diet. So look for them drinking at pools among or near trees. They are often confiding and if you sit quietly, you may be able to study one of evolution's most specialized tools.

While you are in the forest, watch out also for the huge grouse called Capercaillie of which the male in display struts like a turkey, Long-eared Owls hunting the deer runnings, Woodcocks springing out of dense bracken, and other small passerines in the pine and fir canopies. Two of the best are the silver-voiced Goldcrest (Britain's smallest bird) and the black and yellow Siskin, another finch addicted to northern trees, particularly birch and alder.

As the forest yields to heath and that in turn to moss and moor, you should keep a sharp eye for a splendid wading bird. This is the white-backed Greenshank which yells *tewk-tewk-tewk* on take-off and nests in the heather above small marshes. Phil and I found a deer wallow where there were fresh Greenshank prints, but alas we did not see their maker. In the same area, you can put yourself to the test of telling Tree from Meadow Pipit. The former will be in or close to young and scattered trees; the latter will become dominant above the trees. There are plumage differences but the easiest characters to my eyes are the Tree's plumper shape, more buoyant flight, and piercing call *teeze*.

Among the forests and lower moors are many lochans and lochs, all feeding the River Spey. At dawn and dusk, a careful search of some should produce at least long-range views of Goosander which is a large-headed, long-bodied fish-eating duck that nests in treeholes, Tufted Duck whose ducklings appear in late summer, and even perhaps Goldeneye which is now colonizing Scotland. Associated with running water, between the lochs and the river and along the latter, are two other birds that you should try hard for. The first is the longest tailed and most handsomely dressed of all the wagtails, the Grey. The second is the portly, rather thrush-like Dipper. It gets its name from its habit of bobbing up and down on its sturdy legs. Its white chest blazes out from the dark rest of its plumage. Phil quietly stalked a young bird at the outfall of Loch an Eilean and his photograph encompasses its world perfectly. However the most famous bird of the lochs and rivers is the Osprey, a fish-catching hawk that

white in winter

grey-brown in autumn

Ptarmigan

calls rather quiet croaking and grating

NB feathered "snowshoes"

Buzzard

often soars high above forest

call mewing

cock crowing

Capercaillie

Osprey

dark brown above, but mostly white below

adult male in summer

gull-like in flight when far off

flight rapid and true

builds huge nest on treetop

golden back retained in winter, but black shirt lost

Golden Plover

appearance always endearing

Goosander

duck

drake

"sawbilled", like mergansers

delicious trout!

winters in farmland throughout Britain

adult in summer

chick

nests in holes, like Goosander

Goldeneye

drake

duck has wholly brown head and grey flanks

Dotterel

winters in N. Africa

call soft and trilling, unlike plaintive whistle of Golden Plover

orange feet obvious on bird overhead

Siskin

feeds acrobatically
in birches and
alders

hen

cock

wingbars always
striking

cock in flight,
showing sparrow-
like form

Tree Pipit

buffier
than Meadow

calls "teeze"

Crossbill

hen

notes purring,
recalling
Longtailed Tit

young cock,
with many
orange feathers

adult
cock

often suggests
small parrot, due
to bright plumage,
clumsy acrobatics
and large bill

slaking thirst,
caused by diet
of dry seeds

Coal Tit

small, compact, with
unique white spot
on nape

calls "zeee",
quietly,
but often

Goldcrest

Britain's
smallest bird

head pattern less
bold than in other
tits, but crest
unique

Crested Tit

detail of
head and
"hat"

least inclined of
tits to form flocks,
so not easy to find

has successfully re-colonized Scotland in the last 25 years. It is a magnificent creature and thanks to the R.S.P.B., no one who visits the Spey Valley from spring to early autumn need miss it. The signs to the first of now over 20 eyries are widely displayed. It is just north of Loch Garten and can be watched from a hide just off the road. Always stop when you see an Osprey over water; you may be lucky enough to see it dive headlong after a fish.

After a day or two in the valley, forest and foothills, you should be fit (or fitter) for the high tops. So if the forecast is for fine weather, the order of the day can be "climb" and not just "look up". Don't "charge" Scottish mountains; take them steadily along the marked paths. Beware especially of trying to go up along burn and river courses. The going will be rough and the end could be a rock climb, never for amateurs. Once you have breasted a ridge, you can start casting about for the birds of the high tops. Three are worth a special effort. These are the white-winged Ptarmigan which replaces the Red Grouse in the scree slopes and on the barren levels of the massif summit, the chic black-shirted Golden Plover whose wailing cries seem to speak of pre-history, and, in the southern part of the massif, the exquisitely dressed and confiding Dotterel. The last is also a plover and one of Britain's rarest breeding birds. Its breeding behaviour is very unusual because the male is for once the duller of the pair and carries out nearly all the incubating and chick attending duties. Don't disturb any Dotterels that you find. The rule is back off, take cover, and don't overstay your privilege as an observer of a vulnerable species.

You may see other strange birds on the stony summits of the Cairngorm Mountains. If suddenly a sparrow-like bird with much white in the wings, body and lower tail gets up and calls with a lilting *tiddle diddle it*, you have won a major prize in the being of a Snow Bunting. A few pairs of this species breed irregularly. Make it a rule not to ignore any bird on a Scottish mountain. In recent years, the cold springs have apparently provoked breeding attempts by several species that normally breed in Fenno-Scandia. No new Ice Age yet, but definitely a stronger hint of the Arctic!

All the time that you are in deep Scotland, scan the sky. There could be a raptor in it, one of several exciting species from Golden Eagle through Goshawk to Merlin. Phil and I were lucky enough to have a Peregrine go right over our heads.

Juvenile Dipper in first autumn plumage; inspecting its specific food-niche (shallow, running water) from convenient perch near outfall from Loch an Eilean.

Getting there

Exploring Rothiemurchus and the Cairngorms, your base is likely to be Aviemore on the A9. *Après* birdwatching does not have to be different from *après* ski. So why not enjoy all the facilities of the Aviemore Centre? Your approach to the different habitats will only be easy with a car. Buses to anywhere but the ski slopes are things of the past. Because of the precious nature of the country, vehicle discipline is strict. So use only the designated car parks and don't drive off the roads.

Advice on footpaths, weather conditions, ski lift times, nature trails (the one round Loch an Eilean suits all ages), and many other points of interest are freely available from hotels. But the best source is the official information centre at Loch Morlich. If you go on a long traverse of the massif, make sure that someone knows your route. No risks are small if the Scottish weather turns nasty. I know from experience. A "white-out" on the top of Cairngorm nearly had my wife and me permanently parted before we got married!

Walberswick

For marsh birds, especially Bearded Reedling.

From late spring to high summer, few habitats in the world hold more birds than a big reedmarsh; and although the agricultural revolution in Britain has seen the drainage and reclamation of many such areas, a few still exist. This holds particularly in East Anglia. Sadly, water pollution threatens the marsh communities in Norfolk, but those in Suffolk have stayed relatively clean and certainly full of birds. So the choice of a habitat was not difficult, and I chose the one where I first experienced marsh birds and where public access is still largely free of restriction: Walberswick.

Phil and I went there on a dull muggy day in August and did rather badly when it came to actually seeing birds. Most were deep in the reedbeds, busily feeding the last of their broods or recuperating quietly from the maximum effort that successful reproduction requires of birds. So my first piece of advice is, make your visit to a marsh in late spring or early summer. Then the breeding population will be very active, with male songbirds shouting their heads off within their territories and their mates flying around with nesting materials. The larger birds will be evident, too, with idle drakes loafing in bachelor clubs as ducks sit patiently on

Inside of reedmarsh, Walberswick; patiently awaiting for birds along edge of pool, using eyes and ears before glasses.

Old windmill, Walberswick, affording Kestrel perch over pool harbouring rails. Scan the horizon for harriers and Bitterns.

eggs, and with hawks and herons appearing overhead to cause either noisy alarms or quiet dreads. Particularly if you are to find the more secretive species such as crakes and Bitterns, you will need to listen as much as look. Thus your chances are best when all the birds are most using their voices, be they the harsh chatter and swearing respectively of Reed and Sedge Warblers, the weird enveloping boom of a Bittern, the pig-like screams of Water Rails, or the sharp *pzing* of a Bearded Tit. So once again it will be an early rise to make full use of those precious first hours when the natural world is yours alone. 0330 hours is not too soon in late May and June!

An English marsh, rich in cover and food and surrounded by wooded heath, can harbour as many as 120 breeding species; in terms of supporting a diverse and polyglot community of birds, it has no rival in Britain and Ireland. However, as I have already indicated, this ornithological wealth is often masked by the incredibly dense vegetation produced by the dominant plants such as reed, bullrush and sedge. So don't expect to see all marsh birds on one visit. A marsh is no place for the impatient birdwatcher. To tramp about in reeds is a quite hopeless manoeuvre; it is also a very selfish act. You must therefore adapt your finding tactic to the situation. First listen and pick out an area full of bird sounds, then select a line of vision – a ditch or pool edge – and then wait and see what pops out. It could be a real surprise. Once at Walberswick, I was waiting for some beautifully russet and delightfully whirring Bearded Tits to appear. As their small but emphatic noises came close, I expected that as usual I would glimpse one or two sidle up a reedstem and bounce away; but suddenly there were a good fifteen at the base of the cover. Soon they all dropped down on to the mud and pranced about in a most un-titlike manner, their long tails cocked up and waving. As I watched them, it finally dawned on me that they were not really true tits, like the Blue and Great, and that we should call them by their alternate name, Bearded Reedling. In fact they are more closely related systematically to the small babblers of the Eastern Palaearctic than to our common titmice. It was a marvellous moment of comprehension, long vested in others but not in me, and just the kind of event that you should always be ready to enjoy.

During the early breeding season, the list of birds resident within or visiting the marshes at Walberswick and towards Dunwich, the coastal shingle and pools and the beautifully wooded rises inland, is splendidly long. Be on the lookout especially for dark long-tailed Marsh Harriers quartering the inner marsh, large white Spoonbills and several kinds of duck in the reed-fringed pools, aerobatic Black Terns above them, black and white Avocets, chestnut-chested Shelduck and

Coast of Suffolk, between Walberswick and
Dunwich; looking rather barren but far from it.
Expect terns over summer surf, waders all year in
lagoons; buntings and larks around winter weeds.

listen for "boom", then watch for one flying over reeds

always fatter and shorter-necked than Heron

Bittern

Pochard

duck

drake

dives for food

cock

whirring up out of reeds

Reed Bunting

cock

both occur throughout reeds

Reed Warbler

cock in song

churrs more than swears

Bearded Tit

listen for calls, wait for birds to climb up reeds

cock

hen

NB cock's black lorgnette

Water Rail

adult

chick

prancing on ground, like babblers

stripe over eye obvious even in flight

Sedge Warbler

cock in song

swears more than churrs

often appears on edges of pools

long toes to assist movement over fallen reeds

occurs on edge of reeds, in ditches and wet thickets

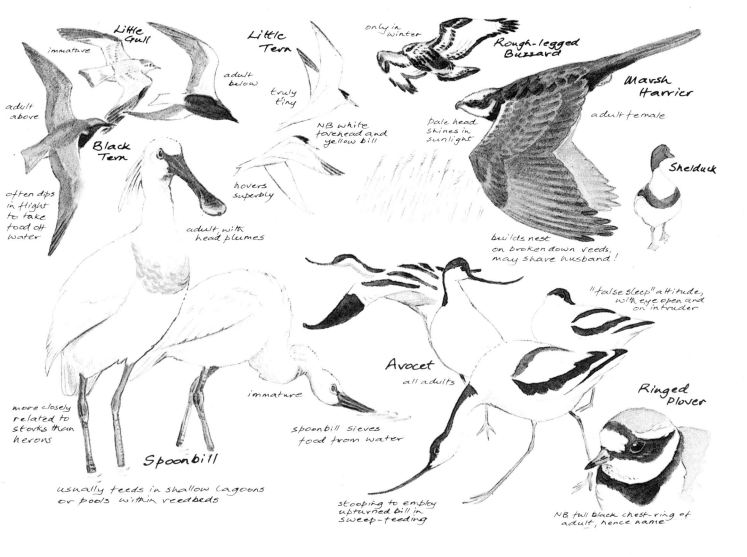

Little Gull

immature

adult above

Black Tern

often dips in flight to take food off water

Little Tern

adult below

truly tiny

NB white forehead and yellow bill

hovers superbly

adult with head plumes

only in winter

Rough-legged Buzzard

pale head shines in sunlight

Marsh Harrier

adult female

Shelduck

builds nest on broken down reeds, may share husband!

Spoonbill

more closely related to storks than herons

immature

spoonbill sieves food from water

usually feeds in shallow lagoons or pools within reedbeds

Avocet

all adults

stooping to employ upturned bill in sweep-feeding

"false sleep" attitude, with eye open and on intruder

Ringed Plover

NB full black chest-ring of adult, hence name

Drainage ditches. Marsh terns fish in them, swifts and swallows take insects above them, and Shelducks graze nearby.

neck-laced Ringed Plovers just inside the coast, and a whole tribe of small birds everywhere. Three of the latter will be difficult to miss, the red-brown Reed Warbler, the even smaller Sedge Warbler with its prominent white stripe over the eye, and the black-headed, white-collared cock Reed Bunting. Take some time with these for they are all key species when it comes to identifying their rarer cousins. Even when you are getting tired feet on the shingle, watch particularly for that hovering fairy, the Little Tern. Once common, this tiny seabird is increasingly restricted to the remaining wilderness. So once you have found one, turn back and leave it in peace.

If you cannot make Walberswick in the spring, then try it in mid-winter. Then the harriers will be ring-tailed Hen, not Marsh; there could be Shore Larks searching the tide-wrack and there will certainly be winter waders among the pools. Best of all, there will be a chance to see a real denizen of the north, the Rough-legged Buzzard. This boldly marked, broad-winged hawk winters more regularly in Suffolk than in any other county.

Finally, if by any chance you make a long journey to Walberswick and are disappointed, never fear. Your journey needn't be wasted since just six miles south is Minsmere, the most famous of all the reserves owned by the R.S.P.B. Particularly if the few Avocets that try to breed at Walberswick are absent, many more are totally dependable upon at Minsmere and you can see them adequately from the public hides erected on the bank that protects the lagoons from the sea. Indeed I shan't blame you for being even more captivated by Minsmere than by Walberswick. It is another magic place for birds but the only way into it is to join the R.S.P.B. and wait patiently for a permit.

Scrub and deciduous wood on north edge of Walberswick marsh; listen in late spring for the beautiful pulsing song of Nightingales.

Getting there

Walberswick is approached by the A12 and an eastward turn down the B1387. About a third of the way into the village, turn back sharp right onto a by-road, and follow this until you see a car park on the northside opposite a broad-leaved wood. Park there and walk down a southward trail leading past the wood to the fringe heath, the reedbeds, and the coastal marshes beyond. You must stay on the dykes, and once past the old windmill you will find those leading first into the centre of the main reedbed and second towards the mounds called the Dingle Hills. If you head straight on, you will end up on the shingle ridge that holds the sea back.

Some of the area is strictly reserved for birds only, so take care to study and follow the notices put up by the Nature Conservancy Council. Remember always that against the flat planes of reedtops and coast, you will be very obvious. So take your time and wait as much as you walk.

North Norfolk

For bird migrants, in the air and amongst the bushes.

There are all kinds of bird studies and it is possible to get as much pleasure and knowledge from watching one as thousands. There is, however, a particularly keen satisfaction to be had from watching large numbers move over a wide horizon, or fall dramatically into coastal cover. The place to experience this is North Norfolk, in late autumn. In spite of various home locations, I still make an annual pilgrimage to experience mass migration along the surf-beaten, sand-blown coast, over the vast saltings and within the tall woods and thickened heaths. The never failing marvel of a long day in North Norfolk is one of the few reasons why I, a pure Scot by blood, can live with being born in Great Yarmouth!

North Norfolk contains Britain's most famous mainland Mecca for birdwatchers. This is made up of the long sand and (cursed) shingle spit called Blakeney Point, the thin reedbeds and lagoons to the east, and the short grass marshes and pools even further east at Salthouse. Collectively they are known as Cley, the place itself being a small village central to the rim of coast just outlined. Since early in the nineteenth century, all sorts of people have watched (and sadly used to shoot) all sorts of birds at Cley, and its fame is such that nowadays the

Coastal flats, dunes and woods, Holkham Gap; watching "visible passage" just after dawn.

Mature conifers and scrub, W. of Wells; often crowded with "fallen" migrants after E. Wind and precipitation.

89

crush of bodies can be too much. So I cannot recommend the area without warning you specifically about the added hazards of frequent disturbance and many more rumours than certain identifications. Indeed I strongly urge that you take your first look at North Norfolk elsewhere, and preferably between Holkham and Morston. Although this stretch of the coast is hugely divided by the river at Wells, the extra miles of tramping bring that measure of solitude that I find so essential to calm and ordered birdwatching.

Phil and I went to North Norfolk on a superb October morning and spent most of our time in the sand dunes and sheltered woods between Holkham Gap and Wells. The dawn sky was as tall as it could be, and as it filled with light many flocks of birds passing east into a westerly breeze became visible. The commonest were Starlings, rushing by in dense murmurations and probably coming from as far away as Poland; with them came Chaffinches from Scandinavia, Lapwings from the Low Countries, and Skylarks from anywhere in north-west Europe. All common birds but all intent on life-saving migration and, as ever, inspiring awe and enjoyment simultaneously. Although the conditions were not ideal, we were given the odd surprise, too. A Great Spotted Woodpecker bounded by, not from tree to tree but overhead at at least 300 feet; a Sparrowhawk flashed in off the sea to be mobbed immediately by the local guardians, a pair of Carrion Crows.

No rarity showed but the astonishingly confident act of mass migration had us both enthralled. This phenomenon can be seen in autumn on many coasts and from inland hill ridges or passes, but the movements over North Norfolk are usually the most obvious and dependable. If you go to see them, try and do so when the wind switches back to west after an easterly spell, and when there is some cloud cover. In fine weather, the birds pass over at great height and your reception of them will be limited to a few tantalizing calls in your ear. To see the movements best, you should get as close to the sea as possible and then look up towards the rising sun for the small silhouettes of the oncoming birds. As these pass

*Juvenile Dunlin in first autumn plumage;
feeding in shallow water mud, into which its bill
probes. Key species in wader identification.*

over or ahead of you, they will become better lit and their identification easier. Remember to use your knowledge of call notes in this situation. Most namings of visible migrants are based on silhouette, flight action, and call (not plumage), and they are amongst the most testing that any observer attempts.

Once you have had your fill of visible passage at Holkham, your next delight awaits you within a few score yards. Searching for grounded migrants is just as exciting as watching others fly overhead, and the chance of putting tabs on a major rarity is actually much better. On several days each autumn and occasionally in spring, the coastal bushes, hedges and woods of North Norfolk swarm with small birds that have drifted in from the North Sea on an east wind laden with fog or rain. In particular, the sallow canopies and bramble patches near Holkham Gap and the birch stands west of the car park at Wells have proved to be almost miraculous in their providence of rare and uncommon birds. Indeed, for all migrants, they offer a much more complete rest area than the dreary sueda bushes of Blakeney Point; and in recent years, birdwatchers have fully demonstrated the amazing ability that bird migrants have of finding the optimum place for recuperation at the end of their flights.

As ever, it is best to be early and take all the light that there is for finding, seeing (which can take long minutes in dense

Reedy pool below Walsey Hill, Cley; haven for tired migrants. In 1975, a Yellow-browed Warbler tried to winter in the pines.

91

Red-breasted Flycatcher

immature

eye-ring prominent

adult

NB frequently cocks tail right up

calls "tzik"

Catches flies in tighter circles than other flycatchers

Pied Flycatcher

hen, cock black where she dun

calls "whit"

NB tail has complete white edges, unlike Red-breasted

NB no obvious pattern in flight

Sparrow Hawk

Chaffinches

distant Starlings

in visible passage along coast

Yellow-browed Warbler

NB long stripe over eye

comes from Siberia!

double wingbar

NB Streaks on crown and chest

no wingbar

Chiffchaff

Sings its name repetitively, from trees in England

blackish legs

cock, in autumn

hen, all year

calls "tzee"

lacks bold marks of Red-breasted and Pied but much commoner and more widespread

Spotted Flycatcher

Redstart

tail flashes red

Sometimes abundant on east coasts after onshore wind and fog

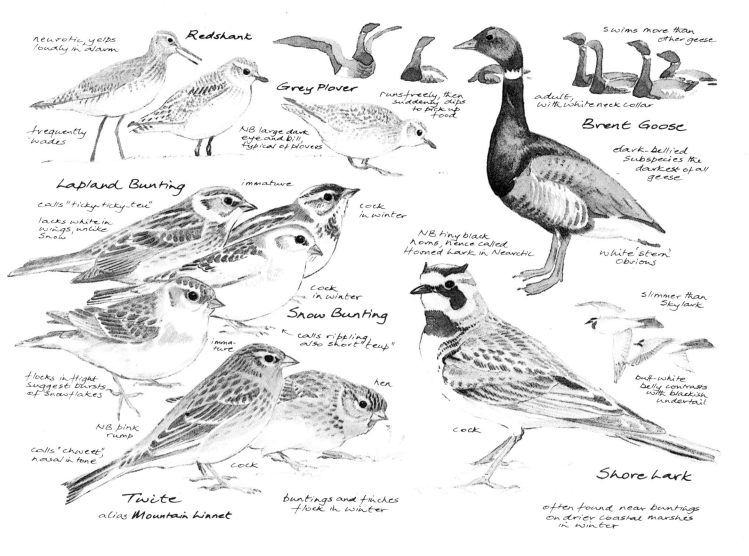

neurotic yelps
loudly in alarm

Redshank

frequently
wades

Grey Plover

NB large dark
eye and bill,
typical of plovers

runs freely, then
suddenly dips
to pick up
food

swims more than
other geese

adult,
with white neck collar

Brent Goose

dark-bellied
subspecies the
darkest of all
geese

white 'stern'
obvious

Lapland Bunting

immature

calls "ticky-ticky-teu"

lacks white in
wings, unlike
Snow

cock
in winter

cock
in winter

Snow Bunting

NB tiny black
horns, hence called
Horned Lark in Nearctic

slimmer than
Skylark

immature

calls rippling
also short "teup"

flocks in flight
suggest bursts
of snowflakes

NB pink
rump

hen

buff-white
belly contrasts
with blackish
undertail

calls "chweet",
nasal in tone

cock

cock

Twite
alias Mountain Linnet

buntings and finches
flock in winter

Shore Lark

often found near buntings
on drier coastal marshes
in winter

cover), and naming. So stroll quietly along the paths, stop at every wing or tail flick, let the bird settle, and concentrate on it or the place where it last went in. In North Norfolk, expert observers know that they may see almost any passerine on the British List (and even one that is not). However on your first visits, you should concern yourself with building up your general knowledge. So work hard on distinguishing the more boldly patterned Pied and Red-breasted Flycatchers from the more homely and uniform Spotted, meeting and enjoying the graceful Redstart whose spread or shivered tail flashes red with an intensity close to electricity, and finding, among the little marked Willow Warblers and Chiffchaffs, that superb sprite that is smaller and covered in stripes. This is the Yellow-browed Warbler, the commonest of all the Siberian and Asian vagrants to reach Britain. Since 1962, I have been lucky enough to see 80 Yellow-browed Warblers and every new one is as delightful as the first. The astonishment that each has flown at least 3,000 miles to be seen is unalterable.

Such birds (and the commoner migrants) only occur regularly in periods of high pressure over Scandinavia or Western Europe. So make good use of the nation's best free service to birdwatchers: the weather forecasts for shipping on radio and for the rest of us on television. Nowadays the latter appear on large maps, complete with satellite photo-

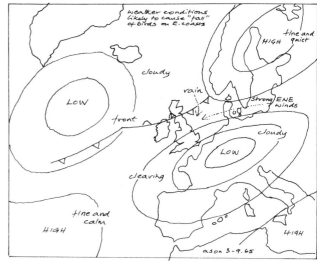

graphs, and you can learn from them the onset of easterly winds, the passage of a rain-bearing front, or the presence of fog. Given these conditions in spring or autumn, the hearts of many birdwatchers are on the east coast or a small island, for just the reasons that I have described.

When in North Norfolk you have had your fill of small birds in the woods (and have not ignored the several excellent residents such as Longtailed and Willow Tits), you can move out into yet another zone of coastal habitats. This comprises both wet and dry saltings, muddy creeks and sandy flats. Amongst these you will find many wading birds such as the Grey Plover from Siberia, whose wingpits are black in all plumages and whose mournful *plee-oo-wee* is perhaps the most instantly recognizable of all wader calls, and certainly the most evocative of wilderness. Inevitably there will be the paranoid yelling Redshanks which all year round will flee from you, removing other birds as they do. From late autumn to early spring, there will also be parties of the dark Brent Goose from Spitzbergen and beyond. Its small size and strange growling chorus may fox you but they are true geese, not large ducks. In the drier areas, take care not to overlook the dull brown Lapland Buntings which will be creeping about and tugging at seed heads like mice, the white-dappled Snow Buntings whose melodic rippling flock calls will turn your head without fail, and the busy groups of warm buff, white-bellied Twites which nest inland on high moors but visit the lowest edges of coastlines in winter. When with them, take care that you are not duped by a bunch of immature Linnets which frequently overlap with Twites in winter. Birds such as these are in North Norfolk for at least seven of the colder months of the year. So you needn't fall into a drain trying to see them all in one autumn day. This is a serious point; soft mud and an incoming tide are no habitat for a human being with boots stuck in a vacuum. Keep an

Immature Starling in first winter plumage; migrant unable to keep up with its flock, so resting on Norfolk bents before feeding and flying on.

95

eye on the sea at all times.

One last point. Among the truly wild birds of Britain, Man has introduced others, sometimes to shoot and eat like the Red-legged Partridge, sometimes to control vermin like the Little Owl, and occasionally to enjoy as ornaments like the Egyptian Goose. All three of these occur in North Norfolk and you should be ready for them, too. The goose is the most unusual but I have often seen it in the fields below Holkham Hall. I find it hard to praise. It looks right only in Africa!

Getting there

All of the places and habitats mentioned can be approached closely by car along side roads or tracks leading north from the A149. Strategic parking is most available at Holkham Gap and beyond the caravan sprawl at Wells. If you are seduced by Cley, be careful on the coastal road there. It is narrow and busy, with an unchecked but clearly high percentage of drivers straining to spot birds before your car. Elsewhere the relevant 1″ Ordnance Survey map is essential map-reading. Driving north from London has become increasingly easy with the advance of the M11 but people coming east from the Midlands should allow for the crawl across the fens on the A17 to Kings Lynn.

Conifer "basement" and coastal bushes, Holkham; former with perches used by migrant flycatchers, latter favoured by breeding and migrant tits and warblers.

Sky above N. Norfolk, with immigrant starlings bounding past on 21 October 1978. Thousands of them and other daytime migrants pass over in late autumn.

A Birdwatcher's Calendar

Although every year brings new experiences and marvellous surprises, its basic ornithological rhythm alters little. Indeed the annual cycle of bird season and changing populations is one of life's most pleasant certainties. I have come to depend on it for more than passing interest and I hope that it will bring refreshment to you, too. To prepare your seasonal enjoyment of birds, I now outline some of the main events of each calendar month and add some hints on what you should do to make the most of them.

Turnstones and Sanderlings, feeding on an English beach in May, soon to fly to the Arctic.

January

Lapwings and Skylarks

The first task for any committed birdwatcher in each New Year is to get rid of the Old. So do not delay the tidying up of your logs, the submissions of records, and any other ornithological matters that will otherwise invoke guilt if left. Then, like me, you will be free for the year that beckons and the birds that it will bring. Many old friends surely, a few new acquaintances without doubt. There may be some decisions to make, too. Changes to main studies, committing to the fatigue of writing them up, involvements in B.T.O. surveys and like issues must all be assessed or your starts upon them will be slow. As an emergent observer, your initial load will not be heavy but be as clear as you can be about the major drives in your interest. Particularly while you are gathering knowledge or acquiring skill, you must think hard about which book to save for next, which great place to visit on your holidays, or where to get some real help on field identification. Planning your birdwatching ahead can save you time and effort. It is also a mouthwatering task for a winter evening.

For birds, January is a month of relative calm, if the

weather is mild, or of almost panic activity, if it is bitter. In the first circumstance, bird movements remain at a low ebb, so there is an excellent opportunity to count the normal winter population of your study area. Miss it and you may have to wait a full year before you get another chance. In the second circumstance, birds may indulge in huge hard weather withdrawals as snow and ice cover their normal habitat and restrict or prevent feeding. So it will always be worthwhile to glance at the sky after a snowstorm. The winter flights of Lapwings, Skylarks and finches can be just as impressive as their autumn immigrations, and there is a chance that they or more unusual birds will turn up right outside your door. Remember though that in any prolonged period of glaciation or wind chill, the deaths of small insectivorous birds like the Wren and other ground feeding species quickly mount. Thus you can contribute directly to their winter conservation by giving them food (but not just pasty white bread) *and* water (very important). Try to do this before dashing off to see what duck have left frozen static waters for open running ones or the inshore sea, and whether Short-eared Owls have entered your local farmland to prey upon the rodents suddenly made dark and vulnerable by white snow.

The occurrence of rare birds in January is usually sparse, though I suspect that this is partly a function of fewer hours of observation in short winter days. Certainly you should always be ready for an uncommon or rare bird and take the opportunity for fame (or notoriety) that it offers.

Later on, I will recommend one birdwatching adventure that relates particularly to each month, but for January I can only urge you to do as much contact as possible with your local habitats and their birds. Make a real effort to know them and your wider excursions during the rest of the year will have much more purpose and relief.

Short-eared Owl

February

Raven

I always feel that this is the coldest month but in a normal British winter (14 out of 15 or so), it is much like January. One non-event is certain; St. Valentine's Day does not find all birds in breathless loving pairs, though some males will begin to sing as the lengthening daylight turns them on a new life cycle. Of this, the first act features a fit male establishing its territory and advertising its tenure and wish to mate.

Any further cold snap, particularly if it is prolonged, will bring in more refugees from Europe. Often the wildfowl and wader populations of Britain and Ireland become noticeably increased as our wetlands act as fall-back zones for many species whose normal winter haunts become frozen over. When the wetlands are full, birds of prey soon come in to attend the wildfowl and select the unfit for consumption. Indeed you may see a sudden Merlin or a majestic Hen Harrier almost anywhere on a cold February day. Conversely any lengthy period of mild weather or even a marked thaw can cause return movements to the east. These are made up of birds eager to regain their normal and re-opened wintering grounds and anxious to escape the greater com-

petitiveness of a doubled-up community. On days of sunshine, the few hardy warblers that winter in Britain show themselves more readily. So be on the look out for Chiffchaff or Blackcap.

In February, a few hardy species commit to breeding. These include Grey Heron and Raven, both of which build large stick nests often prominent in tree tops or cliffs. Watching them at work is most entertaining. The former is not as skilled as the latter but persistence gets it through. The greeting displays that establish the pair bond in Grey Herons are as impressive as those of other large birds. So it will be worth your time to discover the whereabouts of your local heronry and to enjoy the antics. Being confined to the wilder north and west of Britain, Ravens are not so easy to see but you can always find them in the Welsh hills.

Thinking of the last point, I recommend that the first of the year's expeditions should be directed at the Cambrian mountains, and particularly Cors Tregaron. There you can enjoy one of the most legendary birds of the world, the Red Kite. Its attenuated and cruciform silhouette, effortless flight, and richly coloured plumage add up to a supremely beautiful raptor. In winter, there is usually a party of immature birds just south of the town of Tregaron. Once I had several wheeling over my car. Incidentally it is wise to look for uncommon birds of prey in winter. Disturbing them in spring and summer is one of the seven deadly sins of birdwatching. There are few enough left with us without interrupting their attention to a precious new generation.

As in January, rare birds are just that in February; but if you happen to be in the north of Scotland, don't pass any pack of seaducks without a careful scan for King Eider and Surf Scoter. Both are increasing vagrants to Britain and Ireland, the former from the High Arctic and the latter from America.

March

Wheatear

Usually winter ebbs quickly in this month; it is a time of all change in the avian world. I regard the 10th as the start date of my spring birdwatching in England, but those of you who live in Scotland may have to wait another month. As the yellows in the land turn to greens, the winter birds begin to migrate towards their breeding areas and the first of our summer visitors make landfalls. They have come from as far

as Africa and to me the most certain sign of spring is the first cock Wheatear that flashes his white rump over a coastal headland or inland plough. The 15th is not too soon to look for one which has swopped the insect food of the central savannahs of Africa for that of the stony uplands of Europe. He has true beauty, but you may care to debate whether this is not surpassed by the miracle of his safe arrival after 3,000 miles that include the Sahara and two seas. March is the time to anticipate to the south the millions of birds streaming north to the whole of temperate and Arctic Eurasia. At least 55 breeding species are on their way to Britain and Ireland and even if winter whips back for a day or two, you have much to look forward to. Watch particularly for flocks of wildfowl moving north-east in the first half, and many gulls and waders moulting in breeding plumage in the second. If the weather becomes warm in the last week of March, you may expect more than the odd Wheatear to appear. So hold your breath for the first wave of other summer visitors like Willow Warbler and Swallow. Once it breaks, the first signs of the European summer are complete.

Throughout the month, your local birds will start to exhibit breeding behaviour. Tits and Wrens will be inspecting nest holes and the dawn chorus swells daily. Song Thrushes and Blackbirds may well be on eggs by the last week. If you have decided to study a local community, it is high time to make sure that your counting and mapping is organized and begun.

For a real birdwatching adventure, a trip to Islay in March comes second to none. The delights of that bird-filled island have already been described. If by any chance you have had your fill of geese, then concentrate on the other birds.

With many more birds on the move, March produces more rarities than January or February. In recent years, such unusual vagrants as White Stork and Crane have appeared annually and even American ducks like the Ring-necked have popped up among their ordinary British cousins on several waters. It is still rather early for uncommon passerines.

Cranes

April

Hoopoe

Although traditionally the month when English buds burst into flowers and leaves, April has in recent years been colder and wetter than average. Given this, the breeding behaviour of many species may be interrupted or delayed and many winter birds hang on, sensing that their summer ranges may not be open yet. So April can be a very "in-between" month for the birdwatcher. Nevertheless the third or fourth week usually sees the first full flush of summer visitors. Be prepared therefore for that suddenly warm morning when not just hirundines but Swifts are in the sky, and Whitethroats as well as Willow Warblers bounce restlessly in rediscovered breeding habitats. The full return of the small insectivorous birds of summer is an annual miracle and you will find real pleasure in welcoming them back. Few will be the adults of the previous year; most will be only eleven months old. Yet all possess the innate ability to complete a round trip of 5,000 to 6,000 miles and so secure the chance to rear their next generation.

Swifts

House Martin

As the small birds fill up farm and woodland, the larger birds of greater wilderness and coast come in too. Thus any visit to more exposed habitats will find another increasing profile of species, and the potential for your day's list is greater everywhere. To a beginner in birdwatching, spring is an important season. The birds are in relatively fresh plumage with their specific and sexual differences more clearly marked than at any other time of the year. So you must take the opportunity that this affords to apply the disciplines of field identification and build up your experience of each species as it appears. Don't leave this task until autumn. Then moult and wear or immaturity will all add to the problems of diagnosis.

Taking account of what I have just advised, you should consider late April as the best time to make your first visit to a well-managed bird observatory, such as those at Dungeness in Kent or at Gibraltar Point in Lincolnshire. There you can pick up first-class advice on identification, systematic

recording, and the beginnings of a deeper understanding of migration.

As the volume level of immigration and onward passage grows, so does the chance of seeing rare and uncommon birds. If you live in southern England, look out particularly for the incredibly decorative Hoopoe, with its pink body plumage, black and white wings and tail, curved beak and long fan-like crest. It wins all the design awards going!

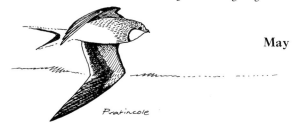

Pratincole

May

In the avian world, the confidence of this month shows promptly after the frequent doubts of April. Even in a late spring, summer visitors pour in or pass by. As the mean temperature rises and holds, the increase in the insect flora means that even the latecomers like Spotted Flycatcher can commit immediately to breeding. The first ten days of May can be marvellously exciting, but the second half of the month sees the settled period for most breeding birds well established. It will last until July. Ducklings appear on ponds and lakes; the fluffy black balls that are young Moorhens trot over lily leaves, and young thrushes scream with hunger. On many shores and cliffs, seabirds are tending their eggs of which some are precariously lodged on ledges little wider than the bird's feet. Thus by the end of May, the breeding population is almost at its peak. I am very chary of nest finding and breathing down the necks of breeding birds but if you do become really interested in studying their activity, there is another book to help you. This is *A Fieldguide to Birds' Nests* by Bruce Campbell and James Ferguson-Lees and I thoroughly recommend it. Remember that if you are studying one particular bird community, it is time for maximum concentration. Otherwise you may miss the shy or quiet species.

If your ear is drawn to bird sounds, May is the month in which to listen to a marvellous variety. The dawn chorus is loud and complex. To a beginner, sorting the owners of all the songs can be a bewildering business. So once again, begin with your local birds and build your knowledge systematically. I suggest you start with the three common thrushes. Learn to tell the rich warble of a Blackbird from the repetitive whistle of a Song Thrush and the wild skirl of a Mistle Thrush, and you will be well on your way to tackling the more difficult vocabulary of the warblers.

The best ornithological adventure in May is a trip to an East Anglian Marsh. You have read a detailed reference to this in the section on Walberswick. Just remember to pick a calm dawn so that you don't lose the magic of marsh sounds, and the birds are not sheltering at the bottom of wind-tossed reeds.

If you must hunt rarities in spring, May is the best month. More than in any month except October, Britain's termination of the Western Palaearctic landmass can be made very obvious by the arrival of vagrants that have overshot the ranges, and occasionally there are great rushes of summer visitors. One such movement is described in the next chapter. Most uncommon birds will occur on the coast or on islands, but you never know.

Dunlins

summer moulting winter

Turtle Doves

June

Most people regard this month as early summer, and most birds do likewise. Some migration remains evident in the first half and Turtle Dove movements can be particularly prominent in the first few days. In general, however, June is the first of two months of relatively calm and warm weather. Since it contains the longest days of the year, it also includes the peak of avian breeding activity. First broods are everywhere out of nests and even immature birds may make some attempt at nest building. Understand that when a whole new generation has to be raised in one season, adult birds have to look to that task and nothing else. Thus with the exception of idle drakes and a few other similar bird husbands, every bird that has successfully paired and hatched eggs is extremely busy stuffing food into voracious nestlings. To witness this concentration of effort, sit by a thicket or near a wooded pool and watch the adults come and go; in with food, out with faecal sacs ("disposable" bags containing droppings, only produced by nestlings), and with rests few and far between. Given an increasing preoccupation with young rearing, the overt territorial behaviour of most species subsides and the volume of song falls quickly.

Robin removing faecal sac

June is essentially a month of regeneration and if you want to understand how organized this can or must be amongst larger birds, go to a seabird cliff and live for a few hours in the nearest thing to a bird city. The section on Flamborough Head explains this more fully. Happily there are many such seabird communities in Britain. I also recommend St. Abb's Head in Berwickshire and Fowlsheugh, south of Stonehaven, in Grampian. Only a little adventure could get you on to the Bass Rock off North Berwick in Lothian. There you can actually walk among the lordly Gannets which nest all over what was the last Jacobite outpost in Scotland.

Rarities are fewer in June than in May but overshooting continues in most years. Most of the species concerned are essentially Mediterranean in origin and the arrival record of such contains marvels like the Beeeater, adapted to do just that and with a plumage soaked in primary colours, and the Roller, fond of beetles and coloured brilliant pale blue and chestnut. Normally you must go to Spain or Greece to be sure of seeing them. So when one turns up in Britain, it makes for a great day!

Finally if your log for the first half year has got rather full, then late June is no bad time to make a first summary of your records. Certainly you must keep up your precision on any census and make sure that you can put the whole of any study of your local breeding population together.

July

Tufted Duck, and family

High summer continues in this month and most birds are still intent on breeding. The small passerines that depend on high productivity of young to withstand the pressures of predation and generally short life spans may well be tending their second or third brood. The larger seabirds are devoting their time to one or two greedy fledglings and the diving ducks now have their ducklings on the waters previously occupied by Mallard and other surface-feeding ducks. Inland the lull in bird movements from mid-June continues and as the late tasks of breeding tax them even more, many birds fall silent. As for us, the birds' year becomes hot, breathless, and quiet. We sometimes tan and peel, they always get worn and ragged.

Two exceptions to the avian *status quo* are the early return movements of northern waders and the build-up on washes and estuaries of other wildfowl. The former can be very interesting, since their members are usually adults in breeding plumage and thus often gay in appearance compared to their drab winter selves. So be on the lookout for such as dusky Spotted Redshanks from Finland and dark-chested Common Sandpipers from Scotland (on inland marshes) and brick-red Bar-tailed Godwits and silver and black Grey Plovers (on coastal flats). Flocks of duck are worth a look too, though much more troublesome to sort out into individual species. With their assumption of an eclipse plumage, drakes look like their mates, and your identification of them will have to be based on structural characters, wing patterns, and flight action. However do not avoid the stern tests involved; they will sharpen your skills.

Early July is the best time for an ascent of the high tops of Britain; the section on the Cairngorms should assist your approach to them. If Scottish mountains seem a bit cold or far, then start with the Derbyshire Peaks or the Cheviots and catch up at least with the marvellous Golden Plover and the majestic Curlew, whose commonest call spells out its name. The long decurved bill of the latter is distinctive. For late July, I also recommend a long watch over a forest, particularly one that is old and broad-leaved. Try and find a vantage point that commands a long horizon of canopy and as the day's air warms and rises in thermals, you can enjoy the hawks exploiting the extra lift and going about their business. In the north and west of Britain, the broad-winged and round-tailed Buzzard should mew above you, and if you are really patient in the south-east, you may be fortunate enough to see a Swift-like Hobby catch a hirundine in full flight. But remember my counsel against close disturbance and accept just their superb silhouettes etched against the blue sky.

Rarities are scarce in July. However, in some years, vagrancy does occur and there could be the odd pink and black adult Rose-coloured Starling or other wanderer to chase. Whilst watching waders, check any puzzling ones carefully. In recent years, a small scatter of American sand-pipers has appeared in July. They are assumed to be mostly birds that have crossed the Atlantic in the previous autumn, have failed to find mates (all an ocean away), and are forced therefore to wander aimlessly.

August

Isabelline Shrike

To most of us, this relaxing month is full of holidays, climax cricket, and sticky peaches; but for birds, it is a different time. Their communities now contain two generations. Tired, worn adults are quietly intent on recovering both fitness and plumage, whilst their eager newly-dressed young dash about improving their innate skills with the trials of independence. For all the summer visitors, their survival also depends on another journey south to the Mediterranean and Africa. This cannot be long delayed and they must lose no time in reaching peak migratory fitness. So birds like chats, fly-catchers and warblers feed hungrily on insects and the new crops of caterpillars and berries in order to lay down the subcutaneous fat that serves as fuel for the first long-haul flight from their summer homes. These long distance migrants have the ability to burn fat as our vehicles consume petrol; alas, no jogger will ever have that! Some groups become exceptionally vulnerable when moulting. The larger wildfowl even become temporarily flightless as they ex-change old for new wing feathers. This is another reason for their seasonal flocking.

Passage from or through Britain can begin as early as late July and certainly by the middle of August, wave upon wave of the small insectivores climb into the mellow dusks of early autumn and, navigating by the stars, fly south. Because of this behaviour, they are often called night migrants. In the second half of the month and particularly if the wind is in the east and mists or rains sweep in from the North Sea, flights of similar birds drift across from Scandinavia and Europe. For the migration student, the 20th is the average date for even greater attention to the weather maps because from then until early November, his most exciting season is open. There are few birdwatchers whose adrenalin does not flush as August approaches September.

In recent years, seawatching from the East Coast has shown that many seabirds hitherto supposed to be regular only in the south-west approaches do occur in the North Sea. So I advise you to try that method of observation first in late August. Fuller details were given in the section on Flamborough Head. Do remember to pick a day of strong onshore wind, and start at dawn.

August is one of the three or four best months for uncommon and rare birds. Usually it provides the first arrivals of American waders that have overflown the Maritimes and the Atlantic, the forerunners of a mob of vagrants from Asia such as redtailed Isabelline Shrikes and very tricky Booted Warblers, and often a small host from Continental Europe. Two are not difficult to enjoy, the strange sinuous Wryneck and the big but usually skulking Barred Warbler. A visit to a bird observatory in the right weather should reward with at least one of these.

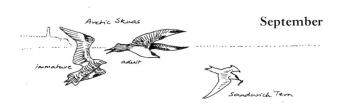

Arctic Skuas

immature   adult

Sandwich Tern

September

In this month the behaviour of our resident birds shows much change. In some families, such as birds of prey, the two generations separate in their search for living room; in others, the tendency to protective flocking increases. There is a move towards winter positions. This is evident in the character of bird emigration, too. The emphasis shifts from the departures of juveniles to that of surviving reclothed adults, while the first arrivals of winter visitors from the north-west and east show the northern tundra and taiga are closing up again. The avian year swings on the equinox and as the days suddenly shorten, it is truly autumn. In some years, bird movements in

September are constant and complex. There may be several widespread falls of drift migrants and resultant onward passages throughout Britain. In such circumstances, birds like Pied Flycatchers and Redstarts can appear almost anywhere. In other years of predominantly westerly winds, small birds are less obvious and it is the turn of waders with their less fickle attachment to traditional routes of passage to catch the birdwatchers' attention.

I find my most fruitful pursuits in September are seawatching and the close inspection of wader flocks. The former activity needs no more explanation. Skuas, those magnificent hawk-like predators of other seabirds, and Sooty Shearwaters, all from the far south of the Atlantic, are visible on most days. The latter activity is important if you are going to meet the two most regular passage migrants from Siberia's marvellous summer stock of birds. These are the endearing Little Stint, the most tiny and active of all common waders, and the elegant Curlew Sandpiper, long-billed as its name

suggests. Look for them to be in company with the abundant Dunlin (another key species in your identification kit) and common Ringed Plovers in sheltered lagoons or on soft mud along the coast. After a major flight, these waders frequently appear on wetlands and floodwater many miles from the sea. If you have an old-fashioned (non-sprinkler) sewage farm or a sandy gravel pit near your home, look there for the product of an Arctic summer in a temperate autumn.

For a day out, I recommend another visit to a bird observatory where birds are trapped for ringing. It will give you the chance to look closely at birds in their first autumn plumage, which is often very different from that worn by adults in winter or summer. You may be lucky enough to see an uncommon migrant in the hand. If it is a green and yellow Icterine Warbler, look closely at the broad base to the bill. This is one of its generic characters and just the sort of clue that you must grasp if your prowess at identification is to grow.

Rarities become relatively common in September. From the middle of the month, it is the time for marvellous sprites like the Yellow-browed Warbler and Red-breasted Flycatcher. To list all the others would take too much space. Check in your field guide for the most likely, and be prepared.

Curlew Sandpipers
in autumn

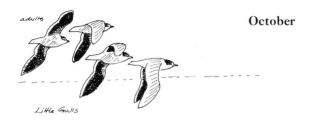

adults

Little Gulls

October

In the birdwatcher's calendar, October never comes too soon. Totally dominated by the phenomenon of migration, it is the most magic month of all. Everywhere in Britain and Ireland birds demonstrate the approach of winter and their need to be in the right place for it. The most visible events are the south-west withdrawals of wildfowl, waders and Starlings from eastern Europe and Siberia, and the arrival of Skylarks and winter thrushes like Fieldfares and Redwings from Scandinavia. Where the warblers and chats of early autumn passed, now swarm Goldcrests and Robins. As the first fingertips of Jack Frost touch such species, their departure from the whole of north-west Europe is hastened and the increasing dominance of low pressure systems makes their migrations more visible. Gone are the fine August nights when birds could fly on and on.

For a wide variety of birds, October holds the prize year after year, and to see a big fall or rush can be a marvellous experience. Islands, headlands, and inland valleys suddenly receive thousands of birds, many literally tumbling out of the sky. Birds become urgent beings totally concerned with survival. Often they cope with even the fiercest gale but occasionally you will see the least fit fail. Such is the rule of natural law. To the coastal birdwatcher, the passage of seabirds continues to be exciting. Huge, hulking Pomarine Skuas appear among their Great and Arctic cousins, and flocks of the charming Little Gull come with south-east gales.

Inland and particularly in any period of Indian summer (increasingly regular in recent years, along with colder springs), the more sedentary species show new plumage and may even begin to sing again. Nevertheless they are still mainly intent on establishing their fitness for winter and staking a claim to a safe haven through it.

For a real adventure in this month, the place to go is North Norfolk, but you can see events similar to those described in the earlier section also in north Kent, at Dungeness, Beachy Head, and Land's End; anywhere indeed where the topography of the land creates a leading line for the birds.

Rarities almost abound in October, and particularly in years of persistent high pressure over the continent and an easterly airflow from Asia, legendary birds appear. Many of these should by rights have gone to Indo China, but a phenomenon known as reversed migration (simplistically young birds reading west from the star map instead of east) causes some to stray up to 4,000 miles off course. These extralimital vagrancies are as remarkable as those of American passerines, and nowhere else in Europe are more proved to occur than in Britain and Ireland. Some of the species that appear have names that identify their long dead discoverers, like Pallas's Grasshopper Warbler and Radde's Bush Warbler. Most systematists say that the latter is a *Phylloscopus* like our own Willow Warbler and Chiffchaff, but to my eyes its behaviour and bill shape point to the minority view which holds it to be in a separate genus. This is just the sort of systematic problem that you may wish to study in due course. One particularly fine bird deserves attention in October. This is the distinguished and fierce Great Grey Shrike. No great rarity but a big brute of a passerine, specialized in the predation of small birds and large insects. Goldcrests beware!

Little Bunting

November

Pallas's Leaf Warbler

This is the month of falling leaves and sinking annuals. Thus the cover for birds both in canopy and over ground is markedly reduced, and with its eclipse goes the bulk of the insect flora. So autumn with all its avian variety and activity rapidly yields to winter. Resident or wintering birds settle in their flocks which become even more obvious as the tactic of being one within a large group is increasingly more protective than the seeking of obscurity in the last patches of dense vegetation. The high tops and other exposed habitats become almost empty of birds. Only a few like the Ptarmigan can stand the coming rigours of snow and ice. Everywhere the task is winter survival.

In most years, the tide of bird migration ebbs fast in November. The numbers of small migrants fall to tardy handfuls, working the last sycamore sprays over and over for insects and grubs. Only the restless thrushes are still common, along with crows, the persistent Starlings, Wood Pigeons and occasional raptors. At sea the chances are no longer of rare shearwaters but of an Arctic gull, like the almost mythical Ross's from eastern Siberia. Particularly when the first ferocious north-easter of the winter howls down the East Coast, a wreck of Little Auks may occur. These tiny cousins to our Guillemots breed in millions in the High Arctic and normally winter in the open seas. Just occasionally hundreds are panicked by extreme frontal weather and so bump on to our coasts. They may even come inland, once even to collide with a cyclist in central London!

Ross's Gull

The expedition that I recommend for November is a return trip to Walberswick or a first visit to another coastal marsh or estuary. If you make one, don't spend all your time on the distant ducks and waders. As I indicated in the sections on Walberswick and North Norfolk, those dark finches along the tide wrack may actually be Lapland Buntings and the larks may be the imperial Shore, not the proletarian Sky.

Rarities become scarce in November but the first half of the month can produce some last chances for them, notably of Pallas's Leaf Warbler which appears significantly later than the Yellow-browed Warbler, and is even more beautiful.

The former led me a most dreadful dance through the late 1960's and early 1970's. While most of my companions were seeing one, two and more, my luck ran solidly bad. In the end, I gave up chasing ghosts and decided that the little beast would have to come to me. Since 1974 it has, four times. God was in his heaven, after all!

December

Smew

If the weather stays wet and not too cold, December sees no great strain put upon birds. A trickle of small bird migration continues in the first two weeks and the sea can still be exciting to watch in any onshore blow. However most birds, whether solitary or gregarious in the winter behaviour, have found their winter niche. If you have chosen a study area, it is best to use early December for another complete winter count. This will allow an assessment of how your own local bird population has fared through the autumn. If you leave your count until later, a cold snap may change the picture with confusing arrivals of birds not normally present.

Once the weather goes cold and particularly if there is a period of snow and frost, the tempo changes. Bird movements both on coast and inland can be quickly visible. In the 1950's and 1960's, this was often the case in the last week of December, and then the majority of birds which use Britain as a fall-back to Western Europe would appear. Typical of such species are two large wildfowl, the Russian Whitefronted Goose (a separate race to the Greenland mentioned in the section on Islay) and the Bewick's Swan. Both regularly winter in England but a sudden increase in their numbers always speaks of snow-covered grass and frozen meers in Holland. The last condition also drives out from the Low Countries a superbly beautiful duck, whose short name delights my mother and other crossword veterans. This is the Smew, of which the drake has the finest plumage imaginable, all snowy white with black face mask, jet necklaces and lacy flanks. It is only common in the south-east of England and it will be well worth your while to search the large reservoirs around London (for example, those near Staines) for it.

True rarities are few in December but it is always possible that one may be associating with the commoner birds of our countryside. So make a point of searching through the flocks of plovers, finches and thrushes, to name only three gregarious families. Not long ago, one lucky observer was given a Christmas present of a cock Siberian Thrush by his local flock of Redwings. It should have been somewhere in south-east Asia but a long wandering flight had brought it to a wormful English field.

Finally before you enjoy the largest of annual human feasts, don't forget the ornithological household chores that I mentioned in January. A New Year will soon begin, but the old one must be tidied up and properly digested!

Great Days with Birds

Throughout the earlier chapters of this book, I have found it hard to resist mentioning actual events in my birdwatching experience. In this chapter, I give up all pretence of impartiality and try to evoke for you the atmosphere of four of my field days, one each of the year's seasons. The descriptions of these days are taken directly from my narrative logs and I have changed them only to improve their legibility (or readability in your case), and to include certain asides essential to your understanding of the events.

I Winter

By the end of 1963, I was approaching a notable ornithological checkpoint in any birdwatcher's life. I was very close to seeing my 300th bird in Britain. (Nowadays the incredible Ron Johns has led several observers through the 400 barrier but 16 years ago, 300 was not bad in anybody's book.) So when I heard that the flock of Whitefronted Geese at the Wildfowl Trust headquarters also contained a truly wild Redbreasted Goose, I became extremely fidgety. I knew this exquisite and charming bird well in wildfowl collections but to see one that had actually flown from Siberia had been a constant hope for many long winters. As the winter weeks passed and work blocked several opportunities to visit Slimbridge, I became increasingly nervous. Would it go before I had my chance? It did not, but even on the day the haul towards it was longer and harder than most. My log tells the story:

"*January 19th, 1964*
SLIMBRIDGE
Up at 0500 and off to Acton to pick up Bob Emmett (complete with sprained knee but as ever raring to go) by 0606. Definite increase in morale due to at last being free to chase one glorious goose. Away due west on the confused A4/M4 but at a constantly slower rate as the weather forecast lost itself and us in first mist and second fog. Became hopelessly disorientated somewhere in south central England and began to fear the day would be spent on a wild goose chase. However Bob counselled persistence; road north from Bristol actually visible. Hopes revived, only to be dashed again at 0920 when Slimbridge reached and local visibility generously assessed at 100 yards.

Out of the car, the first birds to fly out of the fog were three Bewick's Swans [now common at Slimbridge but quite unusual in 1964]. A fair omen but somehow the finding of any rare goose seemed a forlorn hope. Bob decided against too much early hectic limping on one good leg, but I joined a group of other hopefuls. We splashed down to the Dumbles hides. In front of one were 50 Whitefronts, all ghostly in the fog. These became fully departed spirits when an extremely large keeper and a not much smaller spaniel strode by. (Expletive deleted.) This extraordinary piece of behaviour sent my morale crashing and as we retired to the captive wildfowl, I could only raise some thin astonishment at the tameness of the wild Pintail among them and the size of the Collared Dove colony [Slimbridge was an early stronghold of this recent colonist of Britain and Ireland]. The best light of the day was grey and empty.

However we had reckoned without the enthusiasm of Bernard King who, equipped with the magic red pass that allowed him off the public paths, urged action rather than passive defeat. Such a manoeuvre might be profitable so I fell in at the rear of his patrol for a long march round the outside of the New Grounds. Our aim was to check on the goose flocks reported to be in the northern fields beside the Severn. Off we trudged through the flat sheepwalk and across the river meadows towards the muddiest creeks that I know, and from which the tide was just ebbing. My general state shifted from depressed, irritated and clammy cold to depressed, irritated and clammy hot. It was little relieved by chance encounters with two Lesser Spotted Woodpeckers (the smallest and most endearing of those in Britain), a Chiffchaff, a Tree-creeper (which crept briefly up a haystack instead of a tree), and four Kestrels. I could think of only one bird, a small red, black and white goose. As we edged west along the estuary wall, goose sounds did increase. As we came to the edge of the Dumbles, it became obvious that their utterers and many duck were spread in a wide arc ahead of us. We could not risk flushing them so we had to settle for a long cold watch. From time to time the fog rolled back, and our strained eyes revived as they became able to focus on hundreds of Whitefronts and at least a thousand Wigeon. However, try as we could, our only slight success was composed of nine Barnacle Geese. Hardly value for three hours of effort and patience!

By 1400, I was back at the main gate, even hotter and tending to mutter philosophically about the perils of chasing rarities. Bob, with his usual penchant for raptors, had seen a Merlin. Together we went into the enclosures and enjoyed the captives before making the final ascent of the Acrow tower. Once up there, we could see that at last the fog was really clearing. Soon the Dumbles grass marsh appeared below us and there were geese all over it. Since there had been no word of the Redbreast all day, we looked only half-heartedly, and although we saw the Barnacles again and found two Brent Geese among the Whitefronts, they and a total of eighteen Bewick's Swans did little to add a gloss to the day. Surely we had tried and failed. Ah, well, etc.!

Then some unidentified and hideously gleeful idiot

announced that there had been plenty of opportunity to see, nay, study the Redbreast since late morning – for those who had stayed in the hides! Clearly we had been singled out for disaster and my heart sank to unprecedented depths as one after another of eight long searches through the flocks produced no new goose. To cap it all, the sparse daylight began to go. 'We must go,' I said, 'and look, there's the (expletive deleted) keeper again!' But Bob had other ideas, yelling, 'There's a small goose in that flock!' and pointing to the last of several parties coming in from the north-east. Miraculously its members flew on towards us, but on spotting the keeper they turned back and disappeared behind a line of trees. A long moment that mixed a desire to see another human being removed (totally) with a terror of total frustration and a faint conviction that our luck must change, remained very empty of geese. However as I put my telescope on the last tree, the flock swung into view and there in the middle of my eye was the small goose. It looked good and I watched it all the way down. As it landed, its brilliant white flank stripe flashed and there was No. 299 in Britain, my first wild Redbreasted Goose. After enjoying it as much as possible in ten minutes of gathering gloom, we dashed off to compare it with its captive brethren and so clinch the identification beyond all doubt.

Left Slimbridge at dusk, satisfied though hardly gorged,

Red-breasted Goose, among Whitefronts

and groped home through even worse weather."

Some months after this day, I learnt that the keeper was only doing his duty. To us at the time he seemed to be the ultimate ornithological deterrent!

II Spring

Mostly, spring birdwatching is full of happy reunions and the wonders of how well birds have survived the winter or migrations, and how they will fare in the coming breeding season. Very occasionally, however, it can contain a day on which even the greatest events of autumn are matched or eclipsed. Such feature what are called "rushes" and to experience one is to be marvellously entertained.

For the first 35 springs of my birdwatching, I missed out on "rushes"; but in my 36th, it was all very different. My log of the events is rather terse but here at least are the main scenes:

"*May 1st, 1978*
Act I, Scene I.
Up at 0450, wash dishes and away, forgetting coffee flask as usual!

Act I, Scene II.
Arrive at head, drive down to foghorn, and seawatch to little avail; am surprised by arrival of Andrew Lassey at 0625 and make classic error of dividing forces to count Fulmars from two points. Andrew remains on head, braves rain, and has splendid passage go right under him, notching up Longtailed Skua and 2 Sabine's Gulls (all bound for Arctic tundra, west of Greenland in the case of the latter). My only response from North Landing, two miserable blue Fulmars (from northern populations), so am dashed by his news. Morale worsened by unsuccessful attempt to contribute to cigarette market but this fills up 'solid lash' time. No birds visible at Bridlington.

Act I, Scene III.
Rejoin Andrew at head, still smarting but after picking up 3 Bonxies (alias Great Skua), an east Mediterranean Manx Shearwater and a Little Auk (bound for Spitzbergen), feel better. Become frozen by 0915, ponder on going home but decide not to.

Act II, Scene I.
Foghorn starts, retire with throbbing eardrums to North Landing and try hard. Successfully increase morale with another 2 Sabines and a sub-adult Mediterranean Gull. Start to notice small birds new in, e.g. Ring Ouzel and Wheatears. Again ponder on going home, fill up with petrol to do so but decide on 'Old Fall-up' [suffix '-up' ornithological shorthand for *inter alia* covering an area].

Act II, Scene II.
Robins (grey continental birds) by the road, a Bluethroat (bound for Norway) in the first real bush, more Ring Ouzels and thrushes, more Robins and then in the field corner before the wood (called Old Fall Plantation), an explosion of white. Glasses up, heart thumping. Collared Flycatcher? No. Cock Siberian Stonechat? Yes, in total beauty and glory. There at last not a dull immature but a perfect adult in full breeding plumage. Sit down to enjoy it but it's 'leapy'. Soon have to tail it up the dyke. Distractions begin to abound; Wrynecks, Tree Pipits, more thrushes. I smell real birds and my first spring 'rush'.

Act II, Scene III.
Back out to find Andrew and Irene Smith but take long minutes to do so. Car horn useless against foghorn, reduced

to flashing headlamps. They also into small birds. I sense that we should start search for S.S. from Syke's planation. We do so, only to find shootist shooting. Non-event ensues but Andrew produces cock Ortolan (a bunting bound for Sweden) feeding on plough at ten yards. Exhaustion catches up with us all, struggle on to find huge flock of Fieldfares, more Ring Ouzels, Wrynecks, and a Pied Flycatcher. It is all happening.

Act III, Scene I.
Regroup, 'attack' Old Fall for S.S., fail; trudge over to Sykes' to find Yellowhammers and Greenfinches new in alongside the Ortolan. Suddenly falcon appears, suggests Merlin or Hobby but is neither, being in fact a superb sub-adult male Redfooted Falcon. What a day, with birds from Scandinavia,

Siberia and Eastern Europe all together in one place. We trudge on, still worried about the disappearing Stonechat. Suddenly the Redfoot reappears, grips Skylark (to death) and lands to eat it at 40 yards. We watch amazed as Herring Gull tries but fails to rob it and 'excellent lad' mantles (stands proudly over prey with wings extended in heraldic pose), plucks and eats. Then falcon moves off over cliff. We move forward and put 'white explosion' out of nearest hedge. There he is, too. My most beautiful passerine ever, with black head, 'blood spot' chest and white everywhere else. Heady with success, go after falcon, find Skylark feathers but no more of consumer.

Act III, Scene II.
Trudge for head again. See more Wheatears, flush Lapp Bunting. How many more species on this one day? Brief seawatch shows blue Fulmars still passing.

Act III, Scene III.
Make desperate last bid round Northcliffe Farm and Flatmere. Find Wheatears but little else. Almost relieved, since day spent. Have personally seen 89 species during it!"

The wind on this spring day was E.N.E.4 switching to N.E.7, then N.E.4. These directions and strengths combined with poor visibility and the passage of an occluded front produced a miracle of migration that I do not expect to witness again in only a few square miles of an English headland.

III Summer

Persistently addicted to hay fever, I am not really a summer person, and if I do take a rest from birdwatching it is usually in the pollen-rid middle of the year. However when my family lived in Gloucestershire, the summer birds of central Wales did beckon. In 1967, an attempt to see them was initially frustrated by some strange virus that swooped on my wife Karin and myself, but eventually we made the wooded valleys and high tops. The following brief entry from my log encapsulates the first of five magic days:

"*June 20th, 1967*
WALES: Day 1
Recovered from last week's strange lurgy, we drove straight to the Upper Towey valley. Soon after Bwlch, we began to see Buzzards and had no less than 17 in the notebook before Llandovery. By the time we were really in Kite country, we had notched up 48 in the most remarkable concentration that I have ever seen in Britain.

Compared to my memories of the Upper Towey in 1958, the habitat had little changed but young forestry plantations were visible around the head of the valley. Everywhere we stepped down toward the river or up into the hanging woods, small birds appeared to delight us. The dominant songsters were Wood Warblers, the birds shivering with the intense effort of pulsing out their silvery trill so evocative of oak canopy in early summer; but we also enjoyed Spotted Fly-catchers on the lower slopes, Pied above them, Redstarts everywhere and plenty of other warblers, notably chortling Blackcaps and time-ticking Chiffchaffs.

The day filled up with blue sky and warm sunlight and our spirits rose. We saw one very puzzling singleton, a hen Black Redstart just past Rhandirmwyn, but we left it to its secret and climbed up one of the high valleys, hoping for at least a glimpse of Kite. Almost immediately the day's 49th Buzzard appeared and after it came a splendid Kite which was Karin's first in Britain, a hen Sparrow Hawk and, for good measure, a magnificent Peregrine going west. We sat down and just smiled. An array of Britain's best raptors in just over five hours from our sick bed was better medicine than any antibiotic! As we came down, five Ravens flew by – presumably a family party – and a cock Ring Ouzel flashed past. The chorus of Wood Warblers sang on, and by the car a Grey Wagtail took insects from the verge. Wales was doing her best for us, and no mistake.

After such a marvellous opening, we decided not to tarry

kite

and weary it. So we snaked our way through the hill passes to Lampeter. The Buzzard score went to 52, and Pied Flycatchers and Wood Warblers flitted in every wood. After Lampeter, we drove north and up on to the moorland plateau. Immediately the different habitat changed the birds and soon our ears were bathed with the glorious bubbling of Curlews and the indomitable anthems of Skylarks. Two pairs of Stonechat voiced their displeasure at our appearance. Several Whinchats nearby were as ever less truculent. Overhead a 53rd Buzzard appeared.

After a fast downhill run to Tregaron, we voted for some friendly human company and called on Peter Davis and his family in their house overlooking the bog. Outside both flycatchers reappeared, the last two of 55 Buzzards in one Welsh day flew over, and, surprisingly, a duck Garganey flashed its grey forewings over the marsh. Inside Peter showed us the skins of some pureblood Polecats. Some beasts!

To avoid midgies, we went up to Lake Berwyn and camped there. The last birds of a long but fully rehabilitating day were more Whinchats, a Short-eared Owl hunting voles, and some Black-headed Gulls whose raucous voices were not stilled all night!"

In this excerpt from my log, I have disclosed the whereabouts of some of the Welsh Kites. Please take note that this fine raptor remains extremely vulnerable to disturbance. Be content to see it at a distance.

IV Autumn

I thought to face an *embarras de richesse* in choosing a story that would convey the excitement of an autumn day, but in the end one stands out as much as the first of May 1978 does among spring ones. As with my wild goose chase, its eventual triumph was liberally mixed with frustration but the human company was friendly and sympathetic.

In early October 1962, Karin, Bob Emmett and I were manning the St. Agnes bird observatory and with us were James and Esme Ferguson-Lees. We had worked hard to get James away from his then task of editing "B.B." and sceptical as he was (and still is), he was showing signs of accepting the miracles of Scilly birdwatching. This was not surprising after four days of glorious weather and with new rarities, including Britain's fifth Olivaceous Warbler (from Spain) and seventh Lesser Golden Plover (from America), on each of them. However even these riches did not prepare us for what follows. The observatory log reads:

"Thursday, October 4th, 1962
SCILLY
Observers: Same five, surpassing themselves.
Weather: Wing strong S, tending S.S.W. at dusk, when not above f. 3–4; sun most of day but overcast at night.
Birds: ST. AGNES, Part I: A quick check on the Lesser Golden Plover found it still eating earthworms and still on the church plough. Then quickly back to Periglis (the island's harbour cove) for high tide and the wader count. Almost as soon as we got there, a small dark wader popped up only a few yards away. After a few seconds, while his mind recalled his Canadian experience of eight years earlier, D.I.M.W. was extolling the virtues and beauty in miniature of an American Stint [now called Least Sandpiper]. Incredible as it sounds, its appearance was real and after a full hour and a quarter of close observation, all concerned were satisfied with the identification and once again delighted with St. Agnes. The stint was the third American wader of the week but unlike the plover and an emaciated White-rumped Sandpiper (two days before), it was very active, given to much calling and nervous flights. The last of the latter took it off to St. Mary's.
TRESCO: We had already arranged a trip to Tresco and set off in great glee, expecting to find a new wader for Britain. We landed at New Grimsby and were soon scouring the pools and southern beaches. Morning became noon, our feet tired and our spirits sank measurably. We listed 59 species but not one was uncommon, let alone rare. Even D.I.M.W. claimed nothing though he muttered about a duck rather bald on the pate [the alternate name for American Wigeon is Baldpate]. When we all tried for it, the duck got nervous and went off in an aerial circus. Not to have found any rare bird was utterly beyond reason and we all got soaked coming back. Inner thoughts of passing glories depressed.
ST. AGNES: Part II: Still with our fixation with waders, we were back at Periglis soon after 1400. There we added another 'new' wader but it was only a Curlew Sandpiper. Sort of cod roe, not caviar. Then in an offhand manner, the party split up to idle through the northern pieces (small flower fields). R.E.E. and I.J.F.L. had penetrated into the Parsonage Wood when D.I.M.W. and K.A.W. noticed a 'large warbler' darting about in some tamarisk canopy on the edge. Clearly the clumping about of R.E.E. and I.J.F.L. was disturbing it, but D.I.M.W. managed only a strangled announcement of its presence before it plunged out of sight. What on earth was it? This question was answered almost too quickly because suddenly the bird came out on a tamarisk spray, showed a large blob-shaped bill and a striped head and then was gone, tearing across a piece and into deepest hedge. The island echoed to a shout of 'Vireo!' and R.E.E. and I.J.F.L. flew out of the Parsonage. D.I.M.W. recovered

122

sufficient calm to add 'Red-eyed' to 'Vireo' and to assure the others that *now* they had an American passerine to contend with. Then something uncanny happened. The S.S. *Rotterdam*, passing close offshore, saluted the occasion with a glorious trump. We dashed in all directions trying to keep in contact with the delectable American. Its flights were rapid and lengthy but eventually the (more sensible) tactic of watching the Parsonage canopy paid off. We all got excellent views down to a few yards. Sharp-eared I.J.F.L. was able to note its progress through cover by listening for its Willow Tit-like call *tchay*. Not counting a wretched Irish corpse, this is a first for Britain. For this reason and the earlier presence of the exquisite *Calidris minutilla* [the Latin name for American Stint], October 4th has whacked October 2nd into a cocked hat. Who needs *Hippolais* Warblers? (St. Agnes had produced all three found in Western Europe in the previous four days.) As a passing comment we feel that the Peterson drawing of Red-eyed Vireo does our bird no justice. From its erratic behaviour, it was not long in and we suspect that it had jumped ship."

The log of the day went on to describe other migrants and argue that there had been a diurnal fall, surprising in view of the fine weather. On the next day, we found Britain's second Red-eyed Vireo alongside the original bird, and were totally beaten by what can only have been a Yellow Warbler (also from North America). This should have been an absolute first for Britain but its story is so full of frustration, I cannot bear to tell it.

Red-eyed Vireo

Joining National Societies

I have mentioned three universal societies. One other national body deserves mention. You can approach them at the following addresses.

BRITISH TRUST FOR ORNITHOLOGY
Beech Grove, Tring, Hertfordshire, HP23 5NR; Tring 3461. Runs the most scientific and enjoyable conferences, allows you to contribute to science.

ROYAL SOCIETY FOR THE PROTECTION OF BIRDS
The Lodge, Sandy, Bedfordshire, SG19 2DL; 0767-80551. Incorporates Young Ornithologist's Club, gives the best general information and service to a beginner, and manages most of the major bird reserves in Britain.

SCOTTISH ORNITHOLOGISTS' CLUB
21, Regent Terrace, Edinburgh, EH7 5BT; 031-556-6042. Publishes *Scottish Birds* quarterly, organizes regional meetings and annual conference, runs excellent bookshop.

THE WILDFOWL TRUST
The New Grounds, Slimbridge, Gloucestershire, GL2 7BX; Cambridge (Glos) 333. Specializes in the international research and care of wildfowl and flamingoes, maintains several magnificent collections and reserves in Britain.

Reading On

I have already mentioned several helpful books in the text. Here I give you full details of these and add some further suggestions for reading. The list that follows is not exhaustive, but it should be sufficient to maintain a growing interest and to supply most of the facts necessary to a full appreciation of British and Irish birds.

BOOTH, C. GORDON, *Birds in Islay* (Argyll Reproductions, Islay 1975). Excellent example of well-illustrated, neatly written local ornithological guide.

CAMPBELL, B., *The Dictionary of Birds in Colour* (Michael Joseph, London 1974). 1,000 of the world's birds portrayed in colour photographs, preceded by discussion of their systematics related to zoogeographical region and complemented by brief but fact-filled texts.

CAMPBELL, B. and FERGUSON-LEES, I. J., *A Field Guide to Birds' Nests* (Constable, 1972). Fully discusses habitat, nest form and breeding cycle of all birds known to have bred in Britain up to 1972; also describes best method of nest finding for each species.

CRAMP, S. and SIMMONS, K. E. L., (editors), *The Birds of the Western Palearctic*, Volume 1 – Ostriches to Ducks (Oxford University Press, 1977). First part (of seven) of new bible covering all birds in the Western half of Eurasia and North Africa; containing colour plates of all plumages, black and white drawings of displays in many species, and text condensing all current knowledge of each species; expensive but likely to more than hold its value.

MEINERTZHAGEN, R., *Pirates and Predators* (Oliver and Boyd, 1959). Describes the piratical and predatory habits of birds, and also illustrates the leisure and style of past generations of ornithologists.

OGILVIE, M. A., and SHARROCK, I. T. R., "British Birds" Binoculars and Telescopes Survey, *British Birds* 71:10, 429-439. Ask Macmillan Journals Ltd., 4, Little Essex Street, London, WC2R 3LF, for a copy of the October 1978 issue, and (for about £1) obtain the latest advice on your optical investment.

PETERSON, R., MOUNTFORT, G., and HOLLOM, R. A. D., *A Field Guide to the Birds of Britain and Europe* (Collins, 1974). Third edition of classic field guide, incorporating a second series of revisions and all the birds known to have occurred in Europe up to August 1972.

ROBBINS, C. S., BRUUN, B., ZIM, H. S., *Birds of North America* (Golden Press, New York, 1966). Illustrations not quite up to "Peterson" guides, but describes all Nearctic species in one place.

SCOTT, P., *Morning Flight: A Book of Wildfowl* (Country Life, 1935). Beautiful paintings and stories of wildfowling, for when you are bored with maps and identification texts!

SHARROCK, J. T. R., (Managing Editor), *British Birds* (Macmillan Journals). Send £12, for twelve monthly issues, to their Subscription Department, Brunal Road, Basingstoke, Hampshire, RG21 2XS. Worth every penny.

SHARROCK, J. T. R., (Compiler), *The Atlas of Breeding Birds in Britain and Ireland* (British Trust for Ornithology, 1976). "A giant step forward in our knowledge of the distributions of British and Irish birds", containing maps (on a 10 kilometre square grid) of the 218 species found breeding from 1968-1972 and discussion of habitat, nesting behaviour, population rhythm, and size. Includes the Channel Isles.

SVENSSON, L., *Identification Guide to European Passerines* (Naturhistoriska Riksmusect, Stockholm 1975). Handy reminder of basic diagnostic features of birds "in the hand"; useful complement to field guide.

VAN DEN BRINK, F. H., *A Field Guide to the Mammals of Britain and Europe* (Collins, 1967). A good companion to "Peterson" and essential to sorting out some of the mammals that will interrupt your birdwatching.

VOOUS, K. H., *Atlas of European Birds* (Nelson, 1960). All the native birds of Europe portrayed in black and white photographs, complemented by maps of their entire world range and brief life histories.

YEATES, G. K., *Bird Haunts in Northern Britain* (Faber and Faber, 1948). Good example of bird photographer's narrative with plot as well as biology!

Index to Bird References